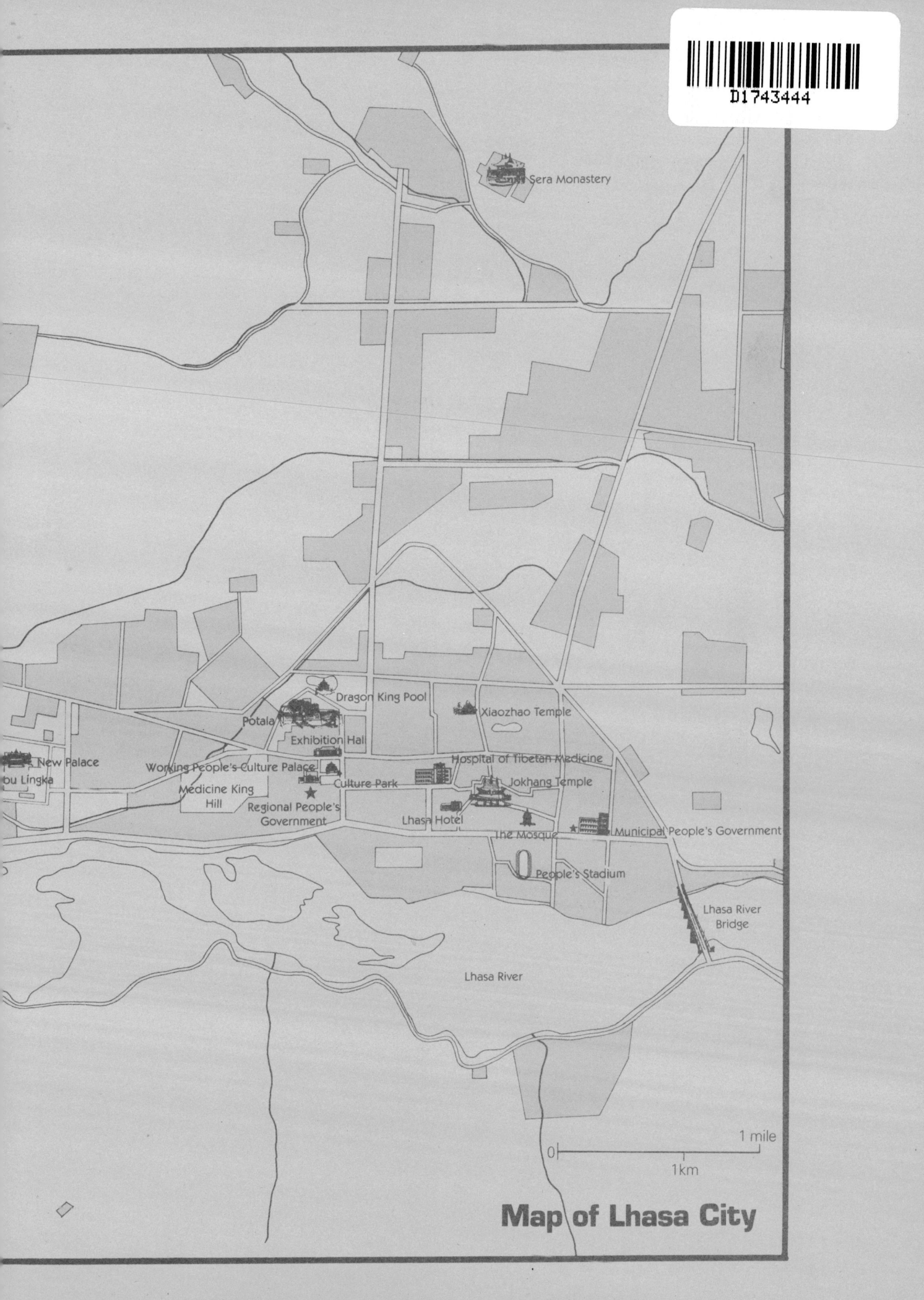

D1743444

Sera Monastery

Dragon King Pool

Potala

Xiaozhao Temple

Exhibition Hall

New Palace
bu Lingka

Working People's Culture Palace

Hospital of Tibetan Medicine

Medicine King
Hill

Culture Park

Jokhang Temple

Regional People's
Government

Lhasa Hotel

The Mosque

Municipal People's Government

People's Stadium

Lhasa River
Bridge

Lhasa River

1 mile

0

1km

Map of Lhasa City

Acknowledgements

This book is published with the valuable assistance and support of the Institute of Nationality Studies, Chinese Academy of Social Sciences.

THE
POTALA of TIBET

THE POTALA OF TIBET

拉宫

STACEY INTERNATIONAL
LONDON AND NEW JERSEY

The Potala of Tibet
Published by
Stacey International
128 Kensington Church Street, London W8 4BH
Telex 298768 Stacey G

171 First Avenue, Atlantic Highlands, New Jersey 07716, USA
Telex 752233 Hilarious

Original edition co-published by Joint Publishing Co. (HK)
and Shanghai People's Art Publishing House, 1982

This revised edition arranged by Joint Publishing (H.K.) Co., Ltd., and
published by Stacey International, 1988

Chinese and English editions © Joint Publishing Co. (HK)
1982, and with Stacey International 1988

Photographed by Zhang Hanyi, Yang Kelin, Li Jun, Dai Jiming,
Kang Song, Yu Pengfei, Li Shuande
Front cover photograph by Nigel Blythe. Back cover photograph by
Sybil Sassoon

Editor
Anthony Guise

Designer
Yin Wen

ISBN 0 905743 48 2

British Library Cataloguing in Publication Data
The Potala of Tibet. – Rev. ed.
Kemp, Richard
    1. Potala Palace (Lhasa, Tibet) – History
    2. Lhasa (Tibet) – Palaces
    I. Title
    951.5   DS786

Library of Congress Cataloguing in Publication Data
    The Potala of Tibet
    Bibliography: p.
    1. Art, Buddhist – China – Tibet. 2. Art, Tibetan.
3. Art – China – Lhasa. 4. Potala (Lhasa, China)
5. Lhasa (China) – Buildings, structures, etc.
1. Kemp, Richard.
N8193.C6P68 1988   704.9'48943'09515   86-14486
ISNB 0-905743-48-2

Set in Garamond by SX Composing Ltd, Essex, England.

Printed and bound by C & C Joint Printing Co. (HK) Ltd.
75 Pau Chung St., Kowloon, Hongkong.

CONTENTS

Edited by Anthony Guise

THE HISTORY OF THE POTALA

by Richard Kemp

THE POTALA PALACE is the most important and impressive example of traditional Tibetan architecture in existence today. More than a third of a kilometre wide, its facade covers the entire face of the Marpo Ri (the Red Hill) which rises above the city of Lhasa, capital of today's Autonomous Region of Tibet, China. Seen from any point on the Lhasan plain, the Potala presents itself as not so much a palace towering on a hill as, magically, a towering hill turned breathtaking palace. With its base sited at more than 3,600 metres above sea level – and with residential apartments a further 110 airy metres above that – the Potala has boasted the most rarefied halls of power the world has ever seen.

Begun in 1645 by Tibet's great 5th Dalai Lama, the Potala as it is seen today has been added to over the centuries by each of his successive reincarnations. The palace complex now comprises a seemingly haphazard maze of more than one thousand rooms of the most subtle artistic workmanship with, altogether, some ten thousand shrines. These, between them, have become a museum to nearly two hundred thousand statues, religious effigies, carvings and figurines. In addition to these the Potala displays murals, tapestries and hanging silks, paintings, parchments, scrolls and sundry scriptures, beside a myriad other *objets d'art* which are almost without number.

The edifice housing this incredible treasure is itself an object of most considerable wonder. Built of wood, stone and earth, its white and burnt-umber walls are dazzlingly sheer. The flying eaves of its shining golden roofs overhang hairpin roads of stone steps which ascend the steep Marpo Ri past fortified towers to the uppermost embrasure of the palace gates.

This spectacle of grandeur and harmony has become a cynosure the world over. The Potala is the icon which, of itself, embodies the strange magnificence and mystery of Tibet's unique religious, artistic, and cultural achievements.

EARLY HISTORY

Tibet's pre-recorded history is one of extreme isolation. Lying behind mountain ranges at more than 5,000 metres above sea-level, the Tibetan plateau is almost a desert and all but inaccessible. As this inhospitable region boasted few natural riches and no obvious wealth, its neighbouring civilizations had no reason to penetrate its fastnesses or to attempt any conquest of its peoples. Owing to their isolation, these people had little in common with the great Asian racial groupings to the north, south and west of their high plateau. In fact, ancient Tibetans believed themselves to be a people apart. Their indigenous myth of genesis told how the union of a monkey with a she-demon created their first ancestors who, as they gradually increased and multiplied, followed rivers down from the mountain of their birth to spread out through the fertile valleys of the habitable earth, thus creating the various Tibetan tribes and peoples.

This myth points to the linguistic and religious cohesion of these Tibetan peoples; but otherwise local isolation and strong clan loyalties divided them completely. Almost all that is known of the region and its history, until the 6th century, derives from the myths and legends which have been handed down from the shamanistic Bon religion which prevailed throughout the highlands at this time. The people only knew themselves by their practice of this religion and called themselves the Bod after it. Elsewhere they were known by rumour as the Bhota, Bhauta or Bauta. Not until the 7th century did Tibetans really emerge from the mists of their legends to become a factually recorded people with sufficient military and economic might to force their highly civilized neighbours into recognizing their existence and further aiding their cultural development.

Tibet owes its national emergence to Songtsan Gambo, the greatest warrior-hero of the Tubo dynastic clan who had long held power in what is now the province of U in the Tibetan heartland. This first truly Tibetan king unified the country's provinces so successfully that he was able to lead the Tibetans down from their remote plateau to challenge the surrounding nations and empires who, until then, had scarcely had cause to care that their mountain borderlands might actually be inhabited.

THE ANCIENT KINGDOM OF TIBET

It was under Songtsan Gambo that Lhasa was transformed from a merely strategic provincial settlement into, first, a national capital and then, soon afterwards, a city of international note. The first reference to a Lhasan palace occurs in the early Tibetan chronicles *Mkhas ba'i dga' stor* (A Happy Feast of the Sages). According to this history, Songtsan Gambo built a fort in the early days of his reign to defend his hold on the town. The fort was sited high on the Marpo Ri hill outside Lhasa and proved to be a most effective stronghold. From here Songtsan Gambo led his forces to unify Tibet; and it was here that he proclaimed himself Tibet's first *tsanpo*, or national king. Some part of this fort still survives in what has now become the Potala's Chogye Drupha (The Meditation Hall of the Religious Lords).

Having established his power at home, the *tsanpo* turned his attention to securing his rule abroad. He sent emissaries to arrange dynastic marriages with the courts of Nepal and China. And although the Nepalese acceded readily enough by despatching a royal princess, Bhrikuti Devi, for immediate marriage in Lhasa, the Emperor of Tang China refused to treat with the Tibetan mission that first arrived to negotiate with his court in 634. But six years later – when Songtsan Gambo had successfully annexed border territories until then tributary to the Tang Empire – the Emperor Tai Tsung proved himself to be more than amenable. When the Tibetan *tsanpo* sent his lieutenant, Gar Tongtsan, to the Tang capital of Chang'an to reiterate his matrimonial request in 640, the Chinese acquiesced by sending Princess Wen Cheng to become his imperial bride. Already renowned as Tibet's greatest military strategist, Gar Tongtsan so impressed the sophisticated Chinese with his brilliant repartee that

Right: *the polished lamellae plumed helmets and fringed coats of Tibetan armour date back to Songtsan Gambo's 7th century reign.*

he received the rare honour of marriage to a Tang princess of his own. And to this day Gar Tongtsan's name remains famous in Tibet as a byword for wit.

However, the cultural achievements of this period do not lie with the king's ministers alone. In the year it took his prospective bride to travel to Lhasa, Songtsan Gambo had time to build a completely new palace on the Marpo Ri to receive not only Wen Cheng and her Nepalese counterpart, but also the three other princesses from Tibet's outlying principalities whom he had already taken to wife. Songtsan Gambo linked this palace to his own fort with a suspended iron bridge and called his now doubly resplendent fortress-palace the Khritse Marpo (the Palace of the Red-Canopied Throne). This fortified palace became the home of Tibet's newly cosmopolitan royal court; within one short decade the Khritse Marpo had established itself as the most brilliant intellectual and artistic centre the country was ever to know.

This extraordinary cultural flowering was as much inspired by Buddhism as it was by the sudden socio-economic stability created by the Tubo regime. Songtsan Gambo's foreign wives were both devout Buddhists by faith. And although the religion was not then entirely unknown in Tibet, popular tradition has long credited these two women with introducing Buddhism to their adoptive country by persuading their husband and king to found the first of its many monasteries and monastic seminaries.

Lhasa's Ramoche Temple with its huge memorial statue to Wen Cheng was certainly commissioned by the Tang princess. She may also have promoted the building of the adjacent Jokhang Temple whose single roof-pavilion the Ramoche shares. The religious images within the Jokhang, still worshipped as the most sacred in all Tibet, were originally brought to the country in the wedding trains of Songtsan Gambo's foreign brides. According to the biography of Wen Cheng depicted in the murals along the corridors and walls of the Potala's vast throne room in the White Palace, the princess retained her personal authority and enjoyed popular esteem long after Songtsan Gambo's death left her a widow in 650. In the next three decades Wen Cheng saw out the reigns of no less than three Tibetan kings and, during this long period of dynastic instability, herself provided sufficient patronage and protection to ensure the survival of Tibet's nascent Buddhist culture.

Tibet also owes its alphabet and the subsequent creation of its literature to the intellectual and religious dynamism of these early years of Tubo rule. In 632, the Tibetan king despatched Tunmi Sangbuza and several other brilliant scholars to Kashmir to learn Sanskrit, study and finally bring home a comprehensive understanding of India's literate civilizations. The date of Tunmi Sangbuza's return to Lhasa is not recorded; however, in less than three decades of linguistic enquiry he had devised thirty characters for an indigenous alphabet which allowed him to transcribe the Buddhist sutras (collections of aphorisms) he had first learned to read in Sanskrit. Tunmi Sangbuza also formulated and fixed the standard grammar, first dictionary and definitive spellings that still determine the modern scribe's use of his or her mother tongue. The first definitive reference to a Tibetan secular text occurs in the ancient annals of Tun-huang, a Chinese city the Tibetans first captured in 787 and controlled for some decades after. These administrative documents refer to the drafting of Tibet's penal code as completed by 655. This official use of the new art of writing dates the introduction to Tibet of a modified form of the Chinese calendar. The massive task of transcribing the entire canon of Buddhist writing into Tibetan may date from Tunmi Sangbuza's own lifetime.

Few, if any, of these very first Tibetan texts and religious translations survive intact among the manuscripts preserved in the Potala's many libraries today. However, the work of canonical translation progressed over one and a half centuries. The Tangeh catalogue, the only surviving record of Tibet's original bibliographic archives, shows a continuing Tubo patronage of Buddhist writing. At least seven hundred Buddhist sutras were transcribed, and possibly taught, under Kings Khride Tsutsan (704-755) and Khrisong Detsan (755-804). A few of these original documents have survived for more than a millennium in the Potala's own archives. Taking their name from the palm leaves on which they are written, these exquisitely beautiful pattra scriptures provide the cultural historian with an invaluable record of the social, as well as religious, conditions of this great age of early Tibet.

The Khritse Marpo has survived rather less well. Established as the seat of real political power in Tibet, the Red Palace, as it had come to be known by the time of its first *tsanpo's* death in 649, became a rather more fortified fort (and correspondingly less pleasant place as a palace) than it had ever been during the security of its founder's reign. According to the famous monk-historian Sumpa Khanpo, the building suffered extensive damage in the dynastic wars that troubled Tibet for the full fifteen years that Songtsan Gambo's young grandson, Mangsong Mangtsan, was ruler (654-669). Sumpa Khanpo's *Dpang bsam lion bzang* (The Precious Tree of Perfect Bliss) also relates that the fortress-palace on the Marpo Ri was badly damaged by lightning in 755, the Year of the Sheep, but was partially renovated and rebuilt sometime during the beneficent years of King Khrisong Detsan's long reign when, militarily at least, Tibet was at its most successful ever. The palace was finally destroyed when the last of the Tubo *tsanpos*, Lang Darma, was assassinated during the general uprising of the Year of the Male Water Dog, 842.

THE MIDDLE AGES

Following the final collapse of the Tubo dynasty in the 9th century, Tibet saw some seven centuries of internecine strife which split the country into small districts dominated by local power factions. During these centuries Tibet was once more held together by religion and language rather than by any coherent national politics. But this time the religion had changed. The successful factions of Tibet's confused Middle Ages are characterized by the close alliance of increasingly dominant Buddhist monastic sects and locally powerful noble families. During these centuries many variant sects emerged, but basically Tibet's Buddhism derived from the mainstream of India's Mahayana Buddhism which had become the Tubo kingdom's state religion in the late 8th century.

Since 791 a pillar at Snagye Temple has proudly displayed Khrisong Detsan's edict proclaiming the Tubo monarchy's official recognition of Buddhism as Tibet's national religion. This monastery had been founded in 755 by the great mystic Padma Sambhava who had come to Tibet at the King's request. Padma Sambhava introduced magical Tantric practices to the country and founded the first of Tibet's great Lamaist sects, the Nyingmapa (The Old School). Khrisong Detsan was anxious, however, that the increasing rivalry of Tibet's established sects would eventually damage his country's national interests. Determined to avert such a potentially disastrous course, this first avowedly Buddhist king caused a theological debate to be staged between 792 and 794 whose outcome would forever determine the precise form of his nation's faith. A Chinese monk (named, confusingly enough, after Mahayana) advanced the cause of the Zen Buddhism then practiced in China as suited to the future of Tibet. In the event, his arguments were overcome by an Indian monk, Kamalasila, who so successfully promoted the Mahayanan theology of moral enlightenment then widespread throughout India, that he persuaded the King to adopt Mahayana Buddhism for his own. However, Tibetan Buddhism cannot be said to have ever remained true to such pantheistic parents as Padma

Right: *detail of a mural illustrating the construction of the Red Palace.*

Sambhava's Tantric wisdom and Kamalasila's Mahayanan teachings; despite Khrisong Detsan's pious efforts, the country fell into political and religious faction fighting that lasted for centuries.

As a result of the complexity of these times, modern Tibetans not only retain much that derives from Chinese Zen, but also accept as integral to their indigenous cosmology some remnants of the pre-Buddhist, shamanistic religion, Bon, which had once dominated the entire country. Bon enjoyed one final, brief resurgence during Lang Darma's rule (836-842, probably). This retrograde monarch's cruel persecution of all Buddhists resulted in a general uprising that saw the extirpation of Tubo dynastic rule. The triumphant Buddhist lamas took care to avoid any further repetition of their own religious persecution. They absorbed whatever remnants of Bon most lent themselves to their own Tantric practices, with the result that friction between the two faiths never again flared into open conflict. Of the Lamaist sects still practising in modern Tibet, the Kagyupa of Tsang Province perhaps remain closest to Bon.

The lamas' policy of peaceful coexistence did not extend to the arena of secular power politics. The clergy vied fiercely among themselves to fill the power-vacuum left by Lang Darma's assassination, and for the next seven centuries Tibet lacked any coherent national consensus. Of the Lamaist sects that came to power during this period, a few, still surviving, are worthy of note.

In 1042 the great Indian teacher Atisa founded the Kardampa sect which stressed the practice of morality and religious discipline leading to enlightenment. In 1080 the Kagyupa sect was founded by a Kardampa monk called Marpa. The Kagyupa's most famous disciple was Milarepa (1040-1123), Tibet's greatest poet. Milarepa's most inspired poems search through Tibet's ancient (Bon) myths and traditions to supply a wholly Buddhist moral teaching. It is thanks to these poems that so much from Tibet's popular oral literature has survived the centuries intact. In 1073 Konchok Gyelpo (an adept Tantric disciple who made use of sexual practices to achieve religious enlightenment) founded the great monastery of Sakya. In the 14th and 15th centuries the Sakyapa lamas rose to prominence. They were closely associated with the Mongolian emperors who, since the time of Ghengis Khan, had dominated China. In 1249 the Mongolian Emperor, Godan Khan, appointed the head of the Sakyapa sect, Sakya Pandita, to rule the provinces of U and Tsang on his behalf; and in 1260 the great Kublai Khan conferred the title of *Ti Sheh* (Imperial Preceptor) on Sakya Pandita's nephew, Phakpa. The Emperor also granted him rulership over all of Tibet's thirteen provinces. It was largely

thanks to Pahkpa's tutelary relationship with Kublai Khan that Lamaism was proclaimed the national religion of the Mongols. And it was within this period that the *Triptaka* (Tibet's Buddhist Bible) assumed the definitive form in which it is written today.

However, the Sakyupa sect was not the only contender for Mongolian patronage. Tusum Khyenpa (1110-1193), the founder of the Karmapa sect, is credited with attempting to convert the greatest of the Mongolian Emperors, Ghengis Khan, towards the end of the 12th century. The Karmapa soon divided into two powerful subsects, the Tsadmarpa (the Red Hats) and the Tsanagpa (the Black Hats). The Tsanagpa introduced the first self-reincarnating High Lama to Tibet, while the Tsadmarpa briefly rose to power in the mid 16th century under the patronage of the Tsangpa rulers of Tsang. During the 15th century the Karmapa's various head lamas became increasingly associated with the Ming emperors who had succeeded the Mongols to China's throne. The Ming dynasty conferred numerous prestigious titles on the Karmapa lamas and lent its patronage to the sect who then held power through large parts of the region on their behalf.

During this century the last and greatest of Tibet's sects came into being. The Gelukpa (those who follow virtuous works) sect was founded in 1403 by a Kagyupa monk, Tsong Khapa (1357-1419). Sometimes called Tsaserpa (the Yellow Hats), the Gelukpa sect sought a return to the Tantric discipline, religious order, and pursuit of moral virtue that had characterized both Atisa's 11th century teachings and Kardampa Geshay's 12th century reformation of Atisa's original Kardampa order. In 1408 Tsong Khapa received an invitation to attend the Chinese Emperor at his court in Beijing. As he was too busy to travel to Beijing in person, Tsong Khapa sent his disciple Jamchen Choje Shakya Yeshe in his stead; he was crowned 'King of Religion' by the Ming court and returned to Tibet a decade later to found the important Gelukpa monastery of Sera in 1419.

The Gelukpa sect produced the Dalai Lamas who were to rule Tibet without opposition from the mid-17th century right up to the modern era. The Mongolian title Dalai (the equivalent of the Tibetan honorific Gyatso, or 'Ocean') was first conferred on Sonam Gyatso by the Qosot Mongol, Emperor Altan Khan. Sonam Gyatso is now reckoned as the 3rd Dalai Lama because he retroactively conferred the title on, first, Gedum Trup (1391-1474) who founded the most important of the Gelukpa monasteries at Trashilhunpo in 1447 and, secondly, on Gedun Gyatso (1475-1542) the first Gelukpa reincarnation to be recognized as such. The 3rd Dalai Lama's reincarnation was recognized in Yonten Gyatso, a great-grandson of

Altan Khan, who was discovered by a Tibetan delegation travelling through Koke Qoto Province in 1601. Yonten Gyatso died young and on several occasions his reincarnation, Ngawang Lobsang Gyatso, had to be protected by Qosot troops from the military might of the Prince of Tsang who supported the many Karmapa intrigues that threatened the Dalai Lama's life. In 1642 the young Dalai Lama overcame the Karmapa lamas and the forces of Tsang with the aid of Gushi Khan. The Qing Emperor approved the Dalai Lama's rule of Tibet and thus assured

Marpo on the Marpo Ri gained awesome significance throughout the country as they became closely associated with the Boddhisattva Avalokitesvara – one of the Buddha's most spiritually pure reincarnations. Avalokitesvara had been Songstan Gambo's patron deity and he had always shared something of his holy lustre; however, the King was more firmly tied to the Boddhisattva in death than he had ever been in life. Legend recounts that Songtsan Gambo merged his being with Avalokitesvara's when his body dissolved into light on his death and his spirit en-

Above: *detail of a mural depicting horsemen competing in the games held to celebrate the completion of the Potala in 1694.*

Tibet's re-emergence as a coherent state enjoying the benefits of strong, central rule. For three centuries the Dalai Lama's Potala Palace has been the synechdotal symbol of their religious rule.

THE TIBETAN RENAISSANCE
During Tibet's Middle Ages the ruins of the Khritse

tered the most holy statue of the saint revered in the Khritse Marpo.

During the political fragmentation of the Middle Ages this twice-holy statue came to stand for the centre of stability that Songtsan Gambo had forged and Tibet had lost. At the same time the destroyed palace of the long-vanished King came to seem a veritable home of the gods. 'Potala' is actually a Tibetan corruption of a Sanskrit place name denoting the hill on the southern shores of ancient India where Avalokitesvara was wont to make his stay. Xuan Zhuang, a Chinese monk writing in the 9th century, transliterated this name as *Po-Ta-Lo-Ka* in his *Datang xiyu ji* (Records of the West Regions of the Tang Dynasty); but this transliteration was quite as commonly contracted to *Po Tuo* by Tibetan monks in whose mother tongue the syllables connote a high place of religious awe.

Thus the 5th Dalai Lama displayed considerable political acumen in choosing to site his new palace on the Marpo Ri and to name it the Potala. The Potala was to stand as a permanent, and massive, reminder of Ngawang Lobzang Gyatso's incarnate descent from Avalokitesvara, and served to tie his own achievement in unifying Tibet with that of Songtsan Gambo. The Potala visibly underscored the Dalai Lama's claim that he and the Tubo King were actually 'two merged into one'. From the outset, then, the palace was not so much designed to provide another hermitage and religious retreat for the Gelukpa sect, as constructed to embody the Dalai Lama's political power.

The 5th Dalai Lama began work on the Potala in 1645. The construction lasted nearly fifty years and was actually completed by Depa (Regent) Sanggye Gyatso, who administered Tibet during the 'interregnum' between the 5th's death and the discovery of the 6th reincarnation. In fact Depa Sanggye Gyatso was forced to conceal Ngawang Lobzang Gyatso's death for some eleven years for fear that his demise would halt construction before the Potala's main portion, the White Palace, could be finished. He announced the Great Fifth's death in 1690 and immediately began work on the Potala's central section, the Red Palace; it took the Regent four years to complete this mausoleum dedicated to housing the Dalai Lama's chorten (sarcophagus).

Together the Dalai Lama and his Depa levied corvée labour from the households of thirteen aristocrats and seven high-ranking officials. This basic source of labour was supplemented by short-term labourers who were called in from monastery fiefdoms and plantation holdings from all over Tibet. These Tibetans also received help from the Chinese Emperor and the King of Nepal who both sent skilled artisans and large numbers of labourers to work for the Dalai Lama. In addition, builders from Kashmir, Sikkim and Bhutan were hired and brought to Lhasa. Not since the court of the Khritse Marpo had the Tibetan capital been so cosmopolitan. All told, a total of 6,743 craftsmen drawn from these various nationalities worked closely together over the half century of the Potala's construction. The 4th Panchen Lama (the second most important Gelukpa leader) sent master mural painters from the Trashilhunpo monastery. Many paintings by the famous Choying Gyatso from Trashilhunpo record the Potala's building process; painters, engravers, founders,

metalsmiths of all sorts, spinners, tanners, stonemasons and mortar-mixers, are all depicted going about their various functions.

Other views of the Potala were left by a handful of Italian Jesuit and Cappuchin monks who entered Tibet and toured through China at intermittent periods during the 17th and 18th centuries. In 1661 a Jesuit priest, Father Johan Grueber, travelled from Beijing with a companion to visit Lhasa and sketched the Potala (then still comprising the White Palace only). This is certainly the first European view of the Potala, and may even be the first pictorial record ever made of it. Fifty years later another Jesuit missionary, Father Ippolito Desideri, visited Lhasa, and was probably the first European to see the Potala much as it appears today. In 1716 he wrote: 'now this palace occupies the whole top of the rock of Potala, but in the old days it was smaller, as shown by the drawings made by the Rev. Albert D'Orville and Rev. Johan Grueber of our society . . .'

Visitors from Beijing also recorded their impressions of the magnificent Potala. In 1720 Li Fengcai (a military officer in the expeditionary force sent by Emperor Kang Xi to expel the Jungar Mongols who had occupied Lhasa and foisted a false Dalai Lama on Tibet) described the Potala in quite some detail as the palace where the Living Buddha was enthroned, and mentioned its many awesome images of worship and its treasuries overflowing with wealth. Jiao Yingqi, a civil officer and Li's close contemporary, visited Lhasa for eight days and, describing the Dalai Lama's magnificent palace in his diaries, wrote of 'hundreds of towering buildings, many storeys high, with beautiful adornments in gold that defy description'; however, Jiao does not mention the Potala by name.

The Dalai Lamas prospered throughout the Qing dynasty (1644-1911) when they enjoyed the patronage and protection of the Qing emperors. The magnificent audience granted the Fifth Dalai Lama by Emperor Shun Zhi when the Tibetan leader visited Beijing in 1652 is indicative of the close, reciprocal nature of this special relationship that lasted for nearly three full centuries. The Great Fifth was greeted with religious deference by the Qing Emperor who reconfirmed his right to bear the title of Dalai Lama that Altan Khan had conferred on his predecessor seventy five years previously. For his part, the Dalai Lama blessed the Qing Emperor and graciously accepted the honour and temporal authority bestowed on him. Thereafter, Shun Zhi's successors proved themselves sympathetic to the Gelukpa reform movement in general, and committed to the cause of the Dalai Lama in particular.

In the early 18th century Tibet was plunged into crisis when Tsangyang Gyatso (the romantic 6th Dalai Lama infamous for his libido and love poetry) was abducted by a Mongolian faction within the Chinese Empire that had become hostile to Tibet's autonomy. The Jungar Mongols proclaimed a twenty five year old monk to be the Dalai Lama's reincarnation and set him up as their puppet in the Potala. In 1720 the Qing Emperor, Kang Xi, came to Tibet's aid by sending an expeditionary force in support of the Gelukpa clergy who had recognized their murdered leader's reincarnation in a small boy born in a place near Litang in Sezchuan Province bordering on Tibet. Kang Xi established two Ambans (representatives from the central government) in Tibet to ensure that Keizang Gyatso's rights to the throne would be well protected during the remaining years of his childhood. At the same time the clergy created the Kashag (the Council of Ministers) and the Yitshang (the Secretariat) to fill the office once held solely by the Depa. These new governmental bodies functioned from within the Potala and for the next century and a half the Ambans worked with them to provide Tibet with a stability it had rarely known during the Dalai Lamas' previous 'interregnum' eras. The Ambans oversaw the fair selection of the 8th to 12th reincarnations, and, when each youth was old enough to take the throne, it was the Amban who presided over the accession ceremony in the Potala's Si Shi Phuntsok Hall. The Ambans also provided a channel of communication between the Dalai Lama's indigenous administration and the Emperor's regime in Beijing. The Qing court was committed to defending Tibet's territorial integrity, and on several occasions Qing troops fought on Tibet's behalf; most notably between 1788 and 1792 when Gurkha armies invaded and overran the country.

This amicable arrangement lasted until the opening years of this century when, in 1904, following a failure to agree on a trading pact, an invading British force under Colonel Younghusband overcame courageous Tibetan resistance and reached Lhasa. Thutan Gyatso, the 13th Dalai Lama, fled before the advancing British and found sanctuary with Emperor Guang Xu and the Empress Dowager Ci Xi in Beijing. The British, meanwhile, remained in Lhasa negotiating with the Dalai Lama's officials who had remained behind in the Potala to supervise the running of the country in his absence. The British wore down these officials' resistance and finally secured their signature to 'The Lhasa Convention', a treaty establishing Britain's right to a garrison in Tibet to protect the trade routes that the military expedition had been sent to open up. Nothing very much came from this treaty, and British involvement in Tibet lapsed. The 13th Dalai Lama returned to Lhasa and provided Tibet with strong leadership until his death in 1933.

MODERN TIBET

Magnificent on the high vantage of the Marpo Ri, the Potala has come to symbolize the religious and political destiny of Tibet. In recent decades the palace has received great consideration from the State Council of the People's Republic of China, and in 1961 the Potala was designated one of the nation's historical sites protected by state legislation. Since that time it has received generous funds each year for its repair and maintenance; this care has ensured the survival of a unique building which is one of the world's greatest cultural museums. Since the early 1980s this museum has been drawing an ever increasing number of visitors. The Potala is no longer the hidden crown of the Dalai Lamas' 'Forbidden City'; it is now a unique museum dedicated to the preservation of Tibet's ancient culture, an unparalleled archive whose resources have been opened up to the world.

Note 1: Today 'Qing' is the preferred transliteration for the Imperial dynasty (c.1644-1911) and is used throughout this book. Some readers may be more familiar with the transliteration 'Ching' which was until recently in common use in the West.

Note 2: The 'Han People' as used throughout this book refers to the peoples of central China.

EXTERNAL VIEWS

The Potala is the ornamental peak for which the incomparable 'Roof of the World' has become most famous. The Potala's special magic is to provide a building which lends grace to a scene of outstanding natural beauty. The palace heights on the Marpo Ri command every view of the Lhasa Valley in which the Tibetan capital stands. The clear air and marvellous sunshine for which Lhasa (the Place of the Gods) is renowned mean that, in its turn, the Potala provides a panoramic focus for miles around.

The Potala's foundations are written into the opening pages of Tibet's recorded history. Early in the 7th century Songtsan Gambo, the first king of unified Tibet, established the strategic town of Lhasa as his nation's capital. In 640 Li Shimin, the second emperor of China's Tang dynasty (c.618-907A.D.), dispatched Princess Wen Cheng to cool his powerful neighbour's insistent desire for territorial expansion. By 641 the Tibetan king had furnished Lhasa with a palace fit for his imperial bride. From then on, Tibetan and Chinese chronicles agree, the town became a wealthy city suited to supplying the needs of the cosmopolitan court at the Khritse Marpo.

Although little now survives intact from this earliest period of construction, the Potala is in fact a grand 17th century reconstruction of the 7th century original. In 1649 the 5th Dalai Lama patterned his new palace (today largely discernible in the whitewash walls of the White Palace) on an ancient mural of the Khritse Marpo preserved in the Jokhang Temple. When Ngawang Lobzang Gyatso died thirty years later the construction was not nearly complete. Fearing that the Dalai Lama's death would halt all building work, the Depa (Regent) Songgye Gyatso concealed his demise for eleven years until the White Palace was finally perfect. After announcing the Great Fifth's death in 1690, the Depa added the central architectural massif of the Red Palace to house the holy Lama's carefully preserved remains. Together these two palaces have been extended and repaired until we see them as they appear today.

General View of the Palace

The Potala takes its name from the most complex association of
King Songstan Gambo with Tibet's patron saint the Boddhisattva
Avalokitesvara who had once made his abode at Mount Potaloka in
ancient India. Tibetan Buddhists have long recognised incarnations
of some vital part of Avalokitesvara's essential being in, variously:
the legendary monkey to whom they trace their ancestry; the king
who unified their country; and the Dalai Lamas who were and are
the living embodiment of their own religious spirit.

In naming his palace after the Boddhisattva's shrine, the 5th
Dalai Lama placed himself and his future reincarnations at the centre

Front View of the Palace

The full extent of the Potala's facade measures more than 360 metres from east to west. The palace's groundplan comprises several large terraces set into the slopes of the hill. Together these terraces cover more than 100,000 square metres of land. The vast walls of the White Palace provide a strong visual contrast to the Red Palace set within its centre. The golden roofs above this central section of the Potala mark the Chorten Halls where the embalmed bodies of eight deceased Dalai Lamas lie in state. The Red Palace also houses the private chapels in which the Dalai Lamas used to pray. The White Palace provided the various apartments for the daily administration of Tibet and the internal running of the Potala's large religious institution. The uppermost of the White Palace's storeys was reserved for the Dalai Lamas' living quarters; far below in the palace's substructure were the dark cells of the country's largest prison. In between these two extremes were the quarters, shrines and classrooms of a monastic seminary, the apartments of innumerable monk-officials, besides many kitchens, storehouses and granaries.

Rear View of the Palace (*above*)

The siting of castles and fortresses on hills is commonplace the
world over, but in Tibet it is a fundamental characteristic of all
monasteries and temples. This hallmark of traditional Tibetan
architecture derives from religious, rather than strategic,
considerations. Pre-Buddhist Tibetans believed their high places to
be the habitation of warrior deities called the Che and the abode of
gods. With some Buddhist modification this ancient belief still
persists. The heads of passes, the crests of hills and the peaks of
traversable mountains are all marked with *laptses* – the running walls
or heaps of stones which respectful travellers add to as they pay their
respects to the Che of each place and entreat each deity to help them
safely on their way. A palace on a hill is protected by the immortal
power of its own *genius loci* – which through the centuries may have
become as Buddhist as a Bhoddisattva. It is not at all unusual for
the founder of even a quite petty palace to become confused with its
protecting spirit in the same way that Songtsan Gambo became
entwined with Avalokitesvara whose Tibetan abode the Marpo Ri
was thought to be.

The Nage Pool and Temple (*opposite page*)

The Potala's foundation stones are set deep into the rocks of the
Marpo Ri from which its walls rise sheer. Local clay dug on site
provided the cement and mortar to bind these massive ramparts
together. So much earth was moved to this purpose that an
unsightly open-cast quarry yawned beneath the completed palace in
1694. The 6th Dalai Lama – a *bon vivant* and writer of shockingly
secular love poetry – flooded this open sore on the Potala's flank and
completed the very pretty picture of the pool he had thus created by
siting the Nage temple on a small isle at its centre. Dedicated to the
Dragon King, this charming *chinois* pavilion shares its name with
the pool's reflecting waters.

(*Overleaf*) **View from the Nage Pool**

Lateral Views of the Potala
Tibetan tradition divides the sky into thirteen layers or storeys, each
of which is home to one of the primordial gods of creation. The
thirteen storeys for which Tibetan architecture is distinctive provide
an earthly imitation of, and religious sermon on, this celestial
structure. The Potala's thirteen storeys (*above* and *opposite page*) rise
through a majestic 117 metres and, whatever the time of day, are
almost more lovely than the skies they reflect.

Ramparts and Roads
The Potala's exterior walls (*opposite page*) are of the cavity variety.
The space between a pair of parallel stone ramparts is filled with
earth and rubble meshed together with strips of willow. These walls
are anything from two to five metres thick. Since Lhasa rests
somewhat uneasily on an earthquake zone, the Potala's ramparts and
retaining walls had molten copper poured into their innermost
crevices to make them yet more solid and proof against small,
recurrent, seismic shocks. Broad roads of stone steps link the
Potala's terraces together and underpin its walls (*above*). The roads
are composed of large blocks of rock capable of withstanding the
stone-splitting cold of Lhasa's high-altitude winter. Their steps
ascend the steep hill in a series of straight flights and hairpin bends,
and are shallow enough for a laden horse to negotiate with ease.

The Round Forts

Two round forts guard the Potala's eastern and western extremities. Since *stod* and *smad* in Tibetan signify 'high' and 'low' as well as 'west' and 'east', the western fort (*above*) is the uppermost of the two, while the eastern (*opposite page*) is the lower. The rounded forms of these paired forts also symbolize the sun and the moon. Tibet's high-ranking officials used to ride their horses along the road guarded by these forts at the rear of the Potala (see page 18 for panoramic vista). When they reached the palace heights at the western fort even the 6th rank of Tibet's high clergy and nobility would dismount and, as a sign of respect to the Dalai Lama, would walk the remaining distance to the White Palace's gates.

The East Gate (*opposite page*)
This is the only portal giving public access to the Potala's central halls.

The Drakhang (*below*)
This western section of the palace is a late addition to the structure of the original White Palace. *Drakhang* means a monk's dwelling or a monastery's chambers. A community of 175 monks was housed here.

Classical Windows
All of the Potala's windows (see *right*)
conform to the traditional design of
Tibet. Their deep embrasures and stout,
overhanging sills protect the shutters
and windows from the worst of the
winter's weather. The narrowing frames
are designed to enhance the apparent
height of the building.

The Deyangshar Terrace
Level with the top of the Marpo Ri at 70
metres, this terrace is set halfway up the
Potala. Its 1,600 square metre surface
area provided the palace with a splendid
plaza for religious rituals. Edifying
performances of theatre and mime,
theosophical debates, mystical songs,
incantatory prayers and dances would be
held here on holy days and other festive
occasions.

PALACE INTERIORS

The simple perfection of the Potala's exterior belies the perfect complexity of its interior. In the three centuries since the 5th Dalai Lama first resided here, the palace has undergone many internal structural alterations producing a maze whose intricacies are now beyond any individual knowing. From 1653 the Potala's State Halls, Chorten Halls, chapels, shrines, administrative and residential apartments functioned as the centre of Tibet's religious and secular authority. Lavish in scale, these rooms display a wealth of decoration that is rich in its detail. Like the original Khritse Marpo, the Potala employed the talents of many foreign artisans and labourers. Architectural motifs from China and Nepal are common throughout the palace; but the discerning will also notice the influence of India, Bhutan and Sikkim in the arrangement and appointments of many rooms. The Potala's magical synthesis of these eclectic elements has produced a structure as unique and singular as Tibetan culture itself.

(*Opposite*) **The Song Ge Guo Corridor** is the principal passageway connecting the Deyangshar Terrace with the major halls and shrines located in the storeys above. Built on a scale to accommodate processions, this lofty corridor is lined with massive pillars supporting elaborately carved beams. Exquisite murals cover the entire extent of its walls.

Benba and Lottery Sticks

Late in the 18th century the Qing dynasty became concerned that Tibet's High Lamas and nobility might favour Mongolian competition for sovereignty over Tibet. Fearing that recognition of the Living Buddha's reincarnation might become tainted by politics, Emperor Chien Lung decreed in 1792 that the true Dalai Lama's reincarnation should be chosen by lottery from among the candidates presented. In 1793 the Emperor presented Tibet with a magnificent gold urn for this purpose. Until 1875, whenever more than one child was deemed a possible reincarnation of the Dalai or Panchen Lama, each child's name was engraved on a small ivory stick and placed in the benba, from which one would be drawn under the Amban's supervision. The child thus selected could then lawfully assume his holy office in a ceremony presided over by the Amban. A duplicate benba in Beijing served in cases where Tibetan delegations were visiting the imperial capital.

The Si Shi Phuntsok Hall
(*top*) dates from the first phase
of the Potala's construction
and is the largest chamber in
the White Palace. All
important state functions and
religious ceremonies were held
here, including the *Sitringasol*
(Ceremony of Enthronment) of
every Dalai Lama dating back
to the late 17th century. These
auspicious ceremonies have
given this, the 'Hall of All
Good Deeds of the Spiritual
and Temporal Worlds', its
name.

**The Chorten Hall of the
Great 5th** (*bottom*) has a floor
space of 680 square metres and
is the largest of Potala's halls.
It was built in the second
phase of construction and was
the first of the Red Palace's
halls dedicated to housing the
holy remains of a Dalai Lama.
The murals in this sacrosanct
chapel depict scenes of
religious enlightenment. One
sequence gives special
prominence to the great deeds
of the 5th Dalai Lama's own
life and includes the 1652
audience with Emperor Shun
Zhi in Beijing among them.

The Gilded Inscription
(*overleaf*) forms part of the rich
decoration of the 5th Dalai
Lama's Chorten Hall. Its
Chinese inscription 'Holy
Fount of the Emerging Lotus'
was dedicated to the memory
of the Great Fifth by Emperor
Qing Long sometime during
the 8th Dalai Lama's reign.

Carved and Painted Pillars
Pillars of a uniquely Tibetan design occur at regular intervals
throughout the Potala's corridors, main halls and principal
apartments. Each pillar's shaft is made of solid stone and faced with
wood. Boards prepared for a particular locality were first carved with
a repeating pattern or religious motif before being bound to their
pillars with hoops of brass; these bound boards were then painted in
place. Manjusri, the Buddha of Wisdom pictured here, belongs to
the pillars along the Song Ge Guo Corridor. The vertical cracks have
opened up through the natural movement of the wood over the
centuries and are superficial only.

Carved Motifs

Although Tibetan art seems realistic, its forms actually express a symbolic or religious significance that is far more real to Tibetans than any mimesis or mere copy of the natural world. The motifs pictured here are particular favourites of many Tibetan artists. The animals express the mystic truth of Tibet's origins and refer to the geographical truth of its terrain. According to the myth of creation, Tibet's various peoples came into being when the first originally homogenous Tibetans came down from Mount Kunlum along the divergent courses of four rivers issuing from the respective mouths of the sacred horse, elephant, peacock and lion stationed on the mountain's peak. These rivers are named after the animals at their fountain. The horse (*bottom left*) represents the Dacho Kebab flowing east; the elephant (*top left*) the Langjan Kebab flowing north to Mongolia; and the peacock (*opposite top*) the Magjia Kebab flowing south into India. The Singjen Kebab which flows west to Ladakh is named after the lion, which, as the symbol of Tibet, also gives its name to the Dalai Lama's throne which these animal carvings decorate. The bird deity (*opposite bottom*) is an especially Tibetan religious motif that recurs throughout the Potala in many variant forms.

40

Lintel

Carved Brackets
The innumerable carved brackets upholding the Potala's ceilings
(*opposite page* and *above*) invariably comprise thirteen interlinked
bands of decoration. No matter what other architectural influences
may show in the brackets, these thirteen bands always symbolize the
thirteen meritorious services that earned Sakyamuni his religious
enlightenment as the founding saint of Buddhism. The brackets'
thirteen bands may also supply a wholly Tibetan subtext in keeping
with the Potala's external symbolism. An early myth recounts that
twelve chieftains of the Tibetan peoples met one of the primordial
sky gods who descended from the heavens at Mount Gyangtho to
become the thirteenth, and divine king of the mortal twelve.

External Brackets: Tibet's forests are symbolized in the ferocious, stylized tigers (*top*) supporting the Potala's roofs. All of the palace's external brackets bear either Buddhist mantras and prayers or a painted image of the Buddha (*bottom*).

The curious pig-nosed bracket system (*middle*) is more than an aesthetic whimsy. These distinctive brackets are found on the golden, uppermost roofs of the Red Palace. Their long snouts serve to reduce the force of the wind, thus protecting the Potala's most exposed and vulnerable surfaces from the worst of any violent weather.

The White Pagoda: this religious altar or *laptse* (*opposite page*) is the oldest structure to have survived on the Marpo Ri. In Songtsan Gambo's time this ancient stone both marked the summit where the hill's warrior god had his home and served as a shrine where the devout Tibetans sharing the deity's hill could pay their respects and earn his goodwill and beneficence. Although the *laptse* still rests on the top of the Marpo Ri, it is actually located well within the Potala's midmost levels.

46

Imperial Seal and Gold Plates
The Ming and Qing emperors habitually issued each reincarnated Dalai Lama with solid gold seals and scriptural plates (*top*) recording the impressive titles the imperial court bestowed on each. The square seals shown here were granted to the Great Fifth in 1652 when Shun Zhi reconfirmed the title of Dalai Lama that the Mongolian Emperor Altan Khan had first bestowed on Sonam Gyatso in 1578. The book of interlinked gold plates records the 11th Dalai Lama's many virtues and titles, and was issued to him in 1841.

Atrium
This light-filled space (*left*) provides a pleasant threshold to one of the Potala's many great halls. Note the rich detail provided by the omnipresent pillars, brackets, religious murals and carvings. These provide a strong contrast to the stark simplicity of the door's simple latch and high sill.

The Sasong Langjie Hall is the highest of the Potala's halls; its name ('The Three Splendid Realms') indicates that it encompasses the Dragon Realm of the Underworld, the Human Realm of the Earth, and the Holy Realm of Heaven. The imperial tablet displayed in the hall (*above*) dates from 1720, when Emperor Kang Xi removed the false 7th from the Lion Throne; it proclaims Keizang Gyatso as the true reincarnation of the 6th Dalai Lama who was murdered in 1706. The portrait behind the tablet is of Kang Xi. The Dalai Lamas used to visit these memorials in the Sasong Langjie Hall during the New Year's celebrations, and on the Emperor's birthday.

Entrance to the Phagpa Lhakhang: this chapel (*opposite page*) is one of the Potala's holiest spots and a rare instance of a building surviving intact from Songtsan Gambo's days. It is named after the most ancient statue of Phagpa Lageshari which it houses. The entryway's gilded plaque, commissioned by Emperor Tong Zhi, proclaims that all who enter the chapel's triple doors stand on 'Blissful Soil Nourishing Miraculous Fruits'.

Entrance to the Great Fifth's Chorten Hall: the multiple doors of this impressive gateway (*below*) match the scale and grandeur of the hall within. Their huge brass hinges and handles are gilded with pure gold. There is a religious text above the central door and the whole gateway is adorned with lotus motifs symbolizing religious purity; the wheel-of-life and other religious symbols can be seen at each flower's centre. The blue-maned lionesses in the topmost tier represent the glaciers of Tibet's mountains, and symbolize the country itself.

The door handles, exquisitely fretted and wrought (*detail left*), are formed in the shape of a double-headed and horned demon; one of the pre-Buddhist pan-daemonium that Padma Sambhava subdued in the 8th century and converted into Defenders of the Faith. The plaits of five lucky ribbons bring good fortune to all who enter.

The Zimchung Nyierh Halls occupy the uppermost storey of the White Palace and have provided the Dalai Lamas with their residential quarters ever since Ngawang Lobzang Gyatso first moved into the Potala in 1648. The Dalai Lamas would religiously preserve their predecessors' private apartments untouched; but otherwise they felt entirely free to renovate, remodel and extend their lovely sunlit halls at will.

The Eastern Sunshine Halls (*above*) were built by the Great Fifth and house his, and his reincarnations', chapels, scripture libraries, audience halls, drawing rooms and private chambers. Each of these apartments is a luxurious as the last. The Dalai Lamas' priceless possessions – the various jewelled or gold and silver objects of their religious office – are all displayed here beside the sometimes mundane accumulations and collections of their secluded private lives.

The inviolate holiness of a Dalai Lama's sacrosanct personage meant that only lamas, officials and attendants above the fourth rank of Tibet's complex social hierarchy could aspire to enter the Zimchung Nyierh's hallowed halls.

Although the Western Sunshine Hall (*left*) was built after 1910 to house the 13th Dalai Lama's living quarters, there is little in the style of its decoration to distinguish either its apartments, or their appointment, from those of any other.

55

Precious Treasures
The superbly wrought teapot (*bottom*) is of solid gold weighing more than four kilogrammes. Its accompanying jade cup sits on a golden stand set with lapis lazuli and is itself topped by an ornamental gold cover inlaid with pearls and other precious stones. The translucent agate and jade bowls (*top*) offer a glimpse of some of the lovely objects on display throughout the Zimchung Nyieilı's apartments.

Residential Chamber

This living room (*above*) has been occupied and used by the Dalai
Lamas ever since the Great Fifth first inhabited the most sunlit of
the hundreds of his palace's halls. The several layers of silk hangings
covering the walls are a common characteristic of the Dalai Lamas'
rooms. Living rooms like this one exude an air of homeliness that
transcends the centuries.

MURALS AND PAINTINGS

The murals adorning the many miles of the Potala's walls provide a gallery of fine art and religious paintings on a scale that dwarfs that of Leningrad's world famous Hermitage. Besides these murals, the Potala boasts a rare collection of ancient scroll paintings which includes 246 priceless scrolls painted with gold.

Two main themes recur throughout these paintings' vast array of subject matter: Tibet's history is represented in the historical portraits, pictorial biographies and visual narratives that feature in so many chapels, corridors and halls; while religious motifs, exemplars, illustrations and topics drawn from Buddhist scripture intermingle freely with these historical images. Most of these murals were painted by 32 Tibetan artists working on each of the palace's completed rooms as the Potala was being constructed. Their original paintings have been retouched or repainted time and again over the centuries. Only comparatively few of the 17th century artists' works have been lost to any overpainting of a completely new mural. Such recent murals as do exist tend to adorn the Potala's architectural renovations or, otherwise, fill the walls that such great artists as Tandzin Norbu or Choying Gyatso happened to leave blank.

No matter from which century, Tibetan artists habitually employ high viewpoints and multiple perspectives in their work alongside lines and colours aligned to the vanishing point perspective of the single plane. Thus almost any of the Potala's murals will present a lively mixture of perspectives side by side on a single surface; in the European tradition such a variety would normally be separated by several centuries at the least. The Tibetan tradition of mixing a single dominant colour with a range of richly contrasting tones adds to the distinctive quality of the Potala's art.

However, the religious subject matter of a painting was far more important to its original Tibetan artist than the aesthetic qualities so much admired today. Most of the subject matter in the Potala's murals has been extensively explained in the religious commentaries stored in the palace's vast bibliographic archives. These paintings and their commentaries provide an invaluable source of information for scholars interested in studying the development of Tibet's social history and the course of Tibetan art.

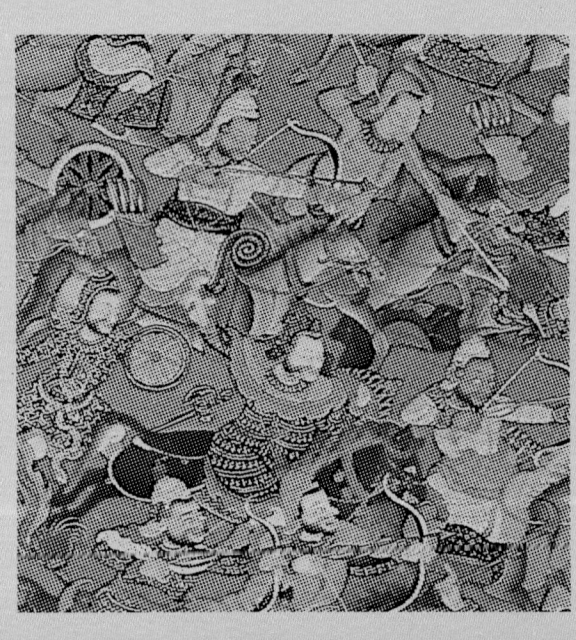

The Great Fifth's Chorten Hall
There are no less than 698 separate panels in the continuous mural
decorating the arcades along this most magnificent Chorten Hall's
first floor gallery (*above*). The mural's many serial scenes depict the
important events of the 5th Dalai Lama's life. The clarity of detail
in these paintings portrays the small lives of quite ordinary Tibetans
alongside the much larger portraits of mighty military leaders and
powerful kings and emperors. The mural's narrative structure
juxtaposes images from Tibet's ancient history with contemporary
episodes from the Great Fifth's own life. These juxtapositions
suggest something of the charismatic leader's national aspirations.
The large portrait of Songtsan Gambo at the centre of the mural
(*overleaf*) reflects the Dalai Lama's self-conscious veneration of this
first Tibetan king.

The Hospitality of Beijing

The detail of the 5th Dalai Lama's audience with Emperor Shun Zhi
in 1652 (*above*) portrays the Great Fifth in the act of blessing the
Qing Emperor. The ritual trappings of Tibetan tea and Qing
hospitality are conspicuous in the painting's foreground. These
elements describe a meeting of mutual accord and reciprocated
goodwill (*First Floor of the Great Fifth's Chorten Hall*).

  The 20th century mural of the 13th Dalai Lama's reception at the
Qing court (*opposite page*) depicts his audiences with the imperial
rulers in remarkably similar terms. The mural's background portrays
Thutan Gyatso at a banquet in his honour given by Emperor Guang
Xu in 1908. The foreground painting portrays the Dalai Lama in
the act of presenting the Empress Dowager Ci Xi with a small
statue of one of Tibet's holy Buddhist images (*Second Floor of the 13th
Dalai Lama's Chorten Hall*).

62

Murals of Ancient Tibet

Many murals provide vivid images of how Renaissance Tibet viewed the first era of its country's ancient history. A copy of the Jokhang's famous mural of the Khritse Marpo (*overleaf, bottom*) depicts Songtsan Gambo's court as a place of peace, plenty and Buddhist harmony. The eponymous red canopy of the Khritse Marpo's throne is topped with a golden turret and flags which, together, are most suggestive of the 17th century Potala's own golden roofs flying a multitude of prayer-flags. Nonetheless, the Tubo palace's fortifications are visible behind the painting's pious reconstructions. Mortared into the flat rooftops of the Khritse Marpo's high defensive towers are wooden imitations of the offensive weapons that, Tibetan chronicles say, were first invented by the primordial sky gods. The bridge suspended from iron chains links the king's palace to that of his consorts. This airy walkway suggests that the Khritse Marpo was as much designed to withstand siege as to provide its inhabitants with any ease of connubial access. This particular painting does not depict the deep trenches elsewhere recorded as an important part of the palace defences; but its flat perspective does emphasize the palace's sheer walls which lack balconies, portals or ledges of any kind except those needed to protect the windows' casements (*Song Ge Guo Corridor*).

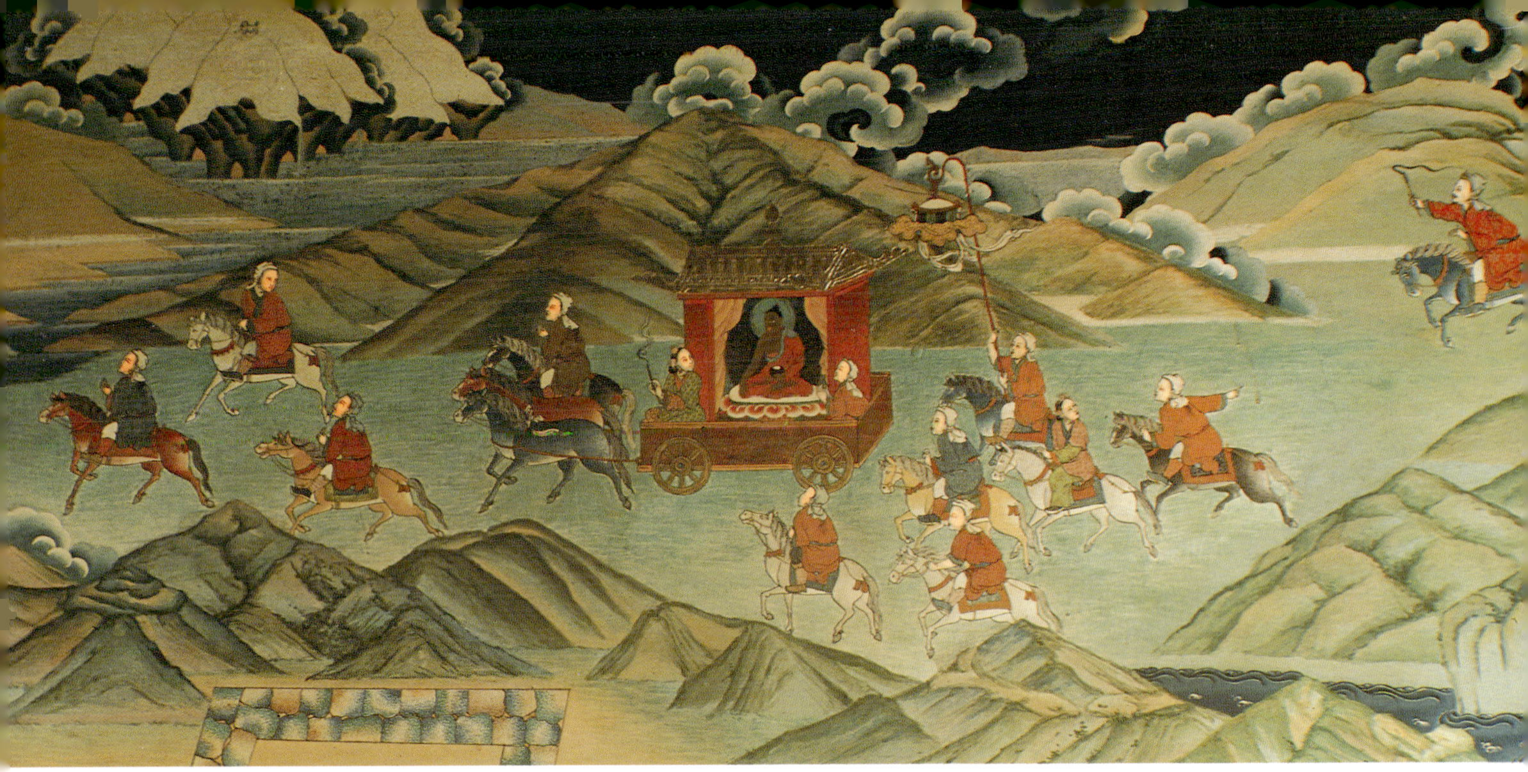

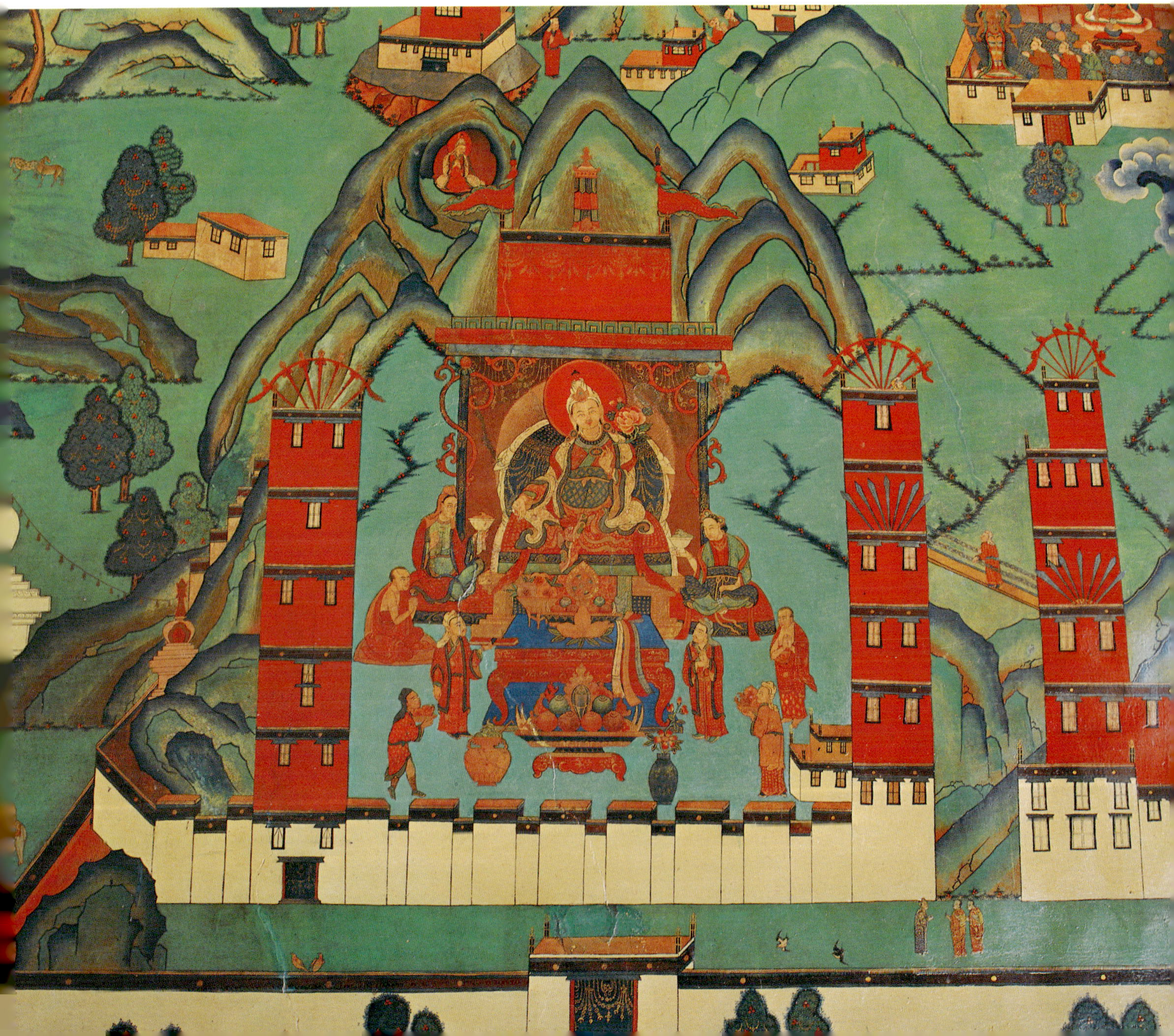

The Tang Princesses

Another mural in the Song Ge Guo Corridor (*opposite, top*) portrays the devout holiness of Wen Cheng, the Tang princess credited with introducing the image of Sakyamuni to her adoptive country. Wen Cheng is depicted *en route* to her marriage in Lhasa. She rides at the exposed front of a carriage whose protective canopy is reserved for the most holy and ancient statue of the Buddha. The riders in the wedding procession include the ink and paper makers, the sericulturists and silk weavers, the millers and brewers and other skilled artisans who, tradition tells, entered Tibet with the Princess to spread their arts and crafts throughout the land (*Song Ge Guo Corridor*).

Elsewhere, another mural (*above*) portrays the highly civilized Tang princess, Jin Cheng, who graced King Khride Tsutsan's court in the 8th century. Jin Cheng was the adopted daughter of Emperor Zhong Zhong and an imperial princess in her own right. She was married to the Tibetan king in 710 and bore his son Khrisong Detsan in 742. This child was to become Tibet's greatest military leader and the country's first officially Buddhist king. Thus Jin Cheng's marriage reconfirmed the ties between the neighbouring Tang and Tubo dynastic houses, added a new impetus to the cultural interchange between the Han and Tibetan peoples, and shaped the kingdom's successful future (*Si Shi Phuntsok Hall*).

Buddhist Deities

The Apsaras (*above*) are minor deities who, serving as the Buddha's attendants, are free to fly through the realms of paradise. The details of this mural are typical of the many sources which simultaneously inform and shape Tibet's Lamaist form of Buddhism. The Apsaras' clothing and stylized gestures are Indian in origin; the dragon roof of the pagoda over which the Apsaras fly is certainly Chinese; and the ice-blue and white clouds which surround them are pure, indigenous Tibetan (*First Floor of the Great Fifth's Chorten Hall*).

These clouds symbolize the limitless creative power of the human mind which has been shaped by religious discipline and holy enlightenment. White tinted clouds, or those imbued with the pastel tints of the rainbow, served many Lamaist monks as an aid to concentrate their meditation.

Such clouds form an important inconographic component of most murals. The many other details visible in the large (5 x 3.5m) portrait of Dhrtarastra, the Heavenly King of the East (*opposite page*), are prescribed by the strict artistic conventions set out by the 14th century in the religious commentaries which together make up the *Tangyur's* holy canon (*Song Ge Guo Corridor*).

Construction of the Red Palace: the mural (*left*) is most interesting for the wealth of information it contains concerning the construction of the Potala and its earliest days as a functioning institution. Materials for the building were transported to the top of the Marpo Ri on the backs of thousands of labourers. Actual work on the walls was accomplished by many small teams of artisans and labourers working in an ordered unison. The completed White Palace was quite clearly fully functional down to the sluicing of its sewers during the final phase of the Red Palace's construction. Monks are depicted at prayer, or are assembled in conclave, when they are not otherwise engaged in theological debate or study of the 'Biblical' *Triptaka's* canons. Artists are also shown painting the many sections of the Si Shi Phuntsok Hall's lovely, lustrous murals.

The Red Palace was begun when Sanggye Gyatso announced the 5th Dalai Lama's death in 1690. Because this building was designed solely to house the Great Fifth's magnificent chorten, its architect commanded that a great stela, or memorial stone, be set up in its courtyard to honour the Dalai Lama's memory during his mausoleum's construction; this still stands where Sanggye Gyatso had it first erected. The detail (*above*) shows how the huge stone for the stela was transported down the treacherous Lhasa River in a cattlehide coracle. The two other coracles in the picture are loaded with rough-cut stones for the palace's construction. The laden porters on the river bank suggest that such water transport was the major route of supply for the vast quantities of materials that entered Lhasa at this time (*First Floor of the Great Fifth's Chorten Hall*).

ཨཿༀ ཕྱི་ཞིང་གི་སྟོང་རས་རབ་ཕུར་ཏེ་རེ་པ་རྫ
ནཔ་བསྐུར་འཛིན་རང་། མོ་ལྷ་བརྒྱར་ནོས་སུ་ཕྱད་

Feats of Horsemanship
Tibetans are fond of
celebrating important events
with games of skill and
daring. This show of
horsemanship is a detail from
the mural depicting the games
Sanggye Gyatso ordered to
celebrate the Potala's final
completion in 1694 (*First Floor
of the Great Fifth's Chorten
Hall*).

Celebratory Games
The many nationalities making up the Potala's artists, artisans and labourers
engaged in good-natured competition during Sanggye Gyatso's massive
celebrations in 1694. Horse and foot races (*top left, bottom right*), weight lifting,
wrestling and archery (*bottom left, top right, top centre*) were all popular events
during the many days of this festival.

Detail from the Shangpala Mythology: Tibetan myths hold that the blessed spirits of legendary Shangpala will assemble in an army led by the epic hero Gesar and come to Tibet's aid in future ages of trouble and barbarity. This army of righteous spirits is painted on a silk roll immaculately preserved in the Potala's fine art collection.

Thangkas of Arhats
Thangka is the art of painting, embroidering or weaving an image on to a cloth or silk scroll. The Potala's thangka collection mainly contains painted scrolls which employ an exquisitely small brush stroke to achieve the flawless finished surfaces (*above* and *opposite page*).

The dominant thangka genre is the depiction of Arhats – those beings whose spiritual perfection through many reincarnations has placed them on a plane approaching Buddhahood. This perfection is most often presented in terms of a formal garden of paradise connected by a narrow bridge to the worldly regions of the earth far below.

SCULPTURES AND STATUES

The Potala houses many genres of sculpture but, in the main, the Buddhist statues in its chapels and shrines constitute the most important and numerous of the entire collection. Statues of such prominent historical figures as Songtsan Gambo, Gar Tongtsan, Tsong Khapa and the Great Fifth are almost a sub-genre of the main religious category. The Potala's halls and chapels provide a solemn and suitably awesome setting for these imposing figures.

Many of the sutras laid down in the *Tangyur's* canon define the iconography and formal rules of composition that bound the artist's execution of a particular figure, no matter whether lay or holy. It would be a mistake, however, to imagine that these prescriptive regulations sought to deny the artist's individual imagination and creative skill. Tibetan art aims to achieve a perfect spiritual truth in its forms and, consequently, uses as much everyday reality as possible to enhance its depictions. Thus most statues will show an animation that speaks of religious conviction and a close observation of life all in one. Often these statues will wear real clothes rather than a painted representation, real jewels rather than imitation. All of this conspires to produce a portraiture that is as readily recognizable as a photographic image.

Such obvious variations as do exist in the depiction of a given subject may be used to date a statue's making. The more Indian or Khotanese a statue's features seem to be, the more likely it is to be ancient. Groupings of statues which impose a vertical or bird's-eye perspective are also likely to be extremely old.

Conversely, a statue displaying obviously Chinese traits most probably dates from Tibet's renaissance and more recent past. Most renaissance statues are cast in either gold, silver or bronze. The older figures tend to be carved in wood or moulded from clay. Certain commanding images measure several metres high, while some of the more miniature figurines are as small as thimbles. No matter what their size, or what the material of their making, the Potala's statues are each and every one a lasting testament to the artistic talent of their anonymous makers.

The Buddha Phagpa Logeshari: this ancient Buddhist image (*opposite page*) is the most holy of the Potala's many holies. Songtsan Gambo is said to have asked the Nepalese for this statue of his patron deity. Legend relates that, at his death, the king's body turned to light when his soul fused with the statue's sacred substance. Popular tradition states that Tibet's own national safety is indissolubly bound up with this statue's own safe-keeping (*Phagpa Lakhang Chapel*).

King Songtsan Gambo (*above*) unified Tibet to make it a sophisticated and powerful kingdom which maintained its national integrity through two centuries of his descendants' dynastic rule. Tibet's socio-political, religious, cultural and economic development is often dated from Songtsan Gambo's reign.

Tibetans regard this king as an incarnation of the Boddhisattva Avalokitesvara. The small image of Amitabha, the Buddha of Boundless Light, emerging from his head-dress signifies the 'father' from whom Avalokitesvara springs and to whom the king owes the incarnate essence of his being. The wavy pencil line moustaches of this figure belong to the royal type established by Khotanese art: its painted robes indicate its great antiquity (*clay, 7th century, 1.55m high*).

Princess Wen Cheng (*above*) was the beautiful, virtuous and highly civilized Tang princess who became one of Songtsan Gambo's five wives in 641. For forty years she provided the nascent achievements of Tibetan culture with a stable centre of royal patronage. Many of the stories handed down about her concern the day-to-day livelihood of the quite ordinary Tibetan people whose hearts she had won. On her death in 680 the Princess was accorded the singular honour of a magnificent funeral; normally the dead were dismembered and left to the birds of carrion, while funerals were the prerogative of kings. Wen Cheng's internment was the equal of her husband's; like his, her body was coated with gold and her treasures spread about her.

Tradition relates that Wen Cheng's and Songtsan Gambo's statues date from the day of their deaths when they were magically created by *phrul* (non-human) craftsmen (*clay, 7th century, 1.11m high*).

Gar Tongtsan was one of Songtsan Gambo's greatest ministers and the most brilliant commander of his armies. Gar Tongtsan escorted Princess Wen Cheng from Chnag'an to Tibet and is famous for the wit which in 641 won him a Tang princess of his own for a bride. With this wife he established a powerful sub-dynasty which flourished for more than a century alongside the Tubo dynasty whose rule he had helped secure (*clay, circa 7th century, 1.8m high*).

(*Above*) Buddhist images in the North Chapel and the West Hall.

Tunmi Sangbuza (*right*) was the scholar who modified the Devonagan script in which he had studied Sanskrit to form thirty letters suited to recording Tibetan speech. This accomplished and prolific linguist produced the *Thirty Rules of Grammar* and the *Lexicological Structure* defining and standardizing the written usage of Tibetan for all time. With its Khotanese moustache and gold tinted skin, Tunmi Sangbuza's statue conforms to the 7th century style modelled on Songtsan Gambo's royal image. This statue's startling blue eyes are, however, quite remarkable. In later centuries such vivid eyes, set in a serene, golden face, came to denote a mortal who had achieved a perfect state of Buddhahood (*clay, 7th century, 1.55m high*).

The established success of this iconography can be clearly seen in the 17th century gold and blue-eyed faces of the many Buddhist images in the North Chapel of the Great Fifth's Chorten Hall (*above*).

The Statue of Sakyamuni (*overleaf, left*) sets the style of sartorial splendour marking all statues cast from the 17th century on. Sakyamuni was the son of King Gautama Suddhodana and heir to the ancient Indian kingdom of Kapilavastu, where he gave up the prerogatives and pleasures of his power to live in the wilderness. There he acquired the religious enlightenment leading to the revealed Buddha. Sakyamuni achieved Pari-Nirvanah, or Buddhahood. His teachings are the founding stone of Buddhism (*gold, 17th century, 2.28m high*).

The Fifth Dalai Lama's Statue (*overleaf, right*) is as revered in Tibet as Sakyamuni's. This statue is cast in silver and its brown eyes incontrovertibly proclaim Ngawang Lobzang Gyatso a Tibetan; but otherwise its inconography proclaims the Great Fifth to be no less holy an incarnation of Buddha than Buddhism's primogenitor (*silver, 17th century, 2.55m high*).

Tsong Khapa was born in 1357 in what is now China's Qinghai Province. Between 1403, when he wrote the two volumes of his great theological treatise, and 1409, when he established the important monastery at Gaden, Tsong Khapa founded the Gelukpa (those who follow virtuous works) sect that was to produce Tibet's fourteen Dalai Lamas and dominate Lamaism. Tsong Khapa's first volume, the *Lam-rim*, seeks a return to monastic discipline, spiritual morality and religious enlightenment through the slow path of virtue characterizing Mahayana Buddhism. His second volume of collected writings, the *Sngags-rim*, is devoted to those intense mental disciplines which can both call the deities into the here and now, and also release the meditating mind from the usual constraints of its physical being.

The statue's clasped hands set Tsong Khapa in the posture associated with Manjusri, the Buddha of Wisdom so much admired by the Gelukpa's Dalai Lamas. The sect's founder was himself a most disciplinarian moderate. Monastic records state that when he visited the Lamaist colleges of logic he 'urged that no-one should engage in running and jumping dances, or the clamour of contemptuous contradiction'. Hearing of Tsong Khapa's reputation as Tibet's greatest theologian, the Chinese emperor invited him to court in 1408. Too busy to go himself, Tsong Khapa sent his disciple Jamchen Choje Shakya Yeshe, who remained there for a decade and returned to Tibet with the title 'King of Religion'. The long association between the Gelukpa Lamas and China's imperial dynasties dates from this period (*silver, 17th century, 2.4m high*).

85

Padma Sambhava (*above*) was summoned from Udayana in northwest India to Tibet late in the 8th century by King Khrisong Detsan. This Indian magician-monk performed miracles and either exorcised or subdued the many Bon demons who then inhabited the land. One history claims the powerful adherents of the native Bon religion drove the troublesome saint out of the country, but most others credit him with founding the great monastery of Samye, fifty miles southwest of Lhasa. He is regarded as the original founding father of the Karmapa sect, and remains the Patron Saint of all

Tibet's non-reformed sects (*silver, 17th century, 2.3m high*).

The White Goddess of Salvation (*opposite page*) is the Tantric goddess revered by most Tibetan Buddhists as the guardian of longevity. The vertical eye in the statue's forehead symbolizes the strange power of her mystical seven eyes. Her omnivision allows the goddess to read people's minds so that no secret can escape her (*gilt silver, 18th century, 1.4m high*).

Incarnations of Tsong Khapa
According to the laws of
Karma, a person's good and evil
deeds determine the spiritual
and material conditions of his or
her next life. A person who has
achieved spiritual perfection
through many lifetimes may
become an Arhat or even a
Boddhisattva before finally
achieving Buddhahood itself.
Such beings are then
reincarnated as a reflexive of
their own perfect goodness to
aid other beings to rise towards
Nirvana. These incarnations are
like reflections of the moon in
the sea. The Buddha is in
Nirvana as the moon is in
heaven, but his incarnations
move across the surface of the
earth in myriad forms just as the
moon's reflection can be seen in
many forms anywhere in the
sea. The Buddha is in Nirvana
as the moon is in heaven, but
his incarnations move across the
surface of the earth in myriad
forms just as the moon's
reflection can be seen in many
forms anywhere in the sea. The
Potala's collection numbers five
exquisitely wrought images of
the various incarnations of
Tsong Khapa. Of the two
shown here, one (*right*) refers
explicitly to the saint's
important national role. The
blue-maned lioness of Tibet
bears Tsong Khapa's incarnation
on her back and gazes up at the
spiritual calm of his face. Once
again, the iconographical
posture associates this saint with
the Dalai Lama's beloved
Buddha Manjusri (*gilt bronze,
17th century, 0.47m high*)

Apex of a Mandorla

The Mandorla is the elaborate frame or halo surrounding a religious image. Mandorlas are richly furnished with elaborate carvings, the most common of which are the Garuda Eagle, dragons and various other bird or serpent deities of symbiosis. The Garuda (*detail above*) is an ancient national symbol and its deific form is frequently found at the apex of those Mandorlas surrounding Tibet's most important saints (*Mandorla: gilt bronze, 17th century; Garuda: 1.1m high*).

Statuette of Maitreya

The Maitreya Buddha is the Buddha of the Future. According to Buddhist doctrine the Buddha incarnate in Gautama is only one of many incarnations to come. The next Buddha will be manifested in Maitreya who will appear on the earth at the end of the *Kalpa* (Buddhist aeon), exactly five thousand years after the birth of Gautama. The fine detail on this statuette of Maitreya (*opposite page*) displays the Tibetans' superb mastery of metal smelting and moulding (*gilt bronze, 17th century, 0.45m high*).

Buddhist Scriptures

The Potala once housed an important theological seminary and the palace today boasts a library of books and scrolls stored in the more than 20,000 surviving compartments of the original college archives. These books span the 1,200 years that have passed since the creation of the Tibetan alphabet. Each book is the work of a monk or a religious thinker. Together the collection covers the canon of Tibetan Buddhism and encompasses such varied subjects as history, geography, linguistics, medicine, astrology and architecture as well as the *ars poetica* from which its volumes of biography, poetry and drama spring.

Certain of the earliest sutras may date from Songtsan Gambo's reign when Sanskrit writings were first translated into Tibetan. Some few more certainly date from Khride Tsutsan's reign when a number of Chinese sutras were translated with the King's own patronage. Many more date from the middle to late 8th century when Khrisong Detsan actively promoted the writing and dissemination of Buddhist sutras in his campaign to counteract the power and practice of the Bon religion in Tibet. The Tangeh catalogue of the 8th century court's contemporary archives lists some 700 such documents of Buddhist scripture. Although most of these are now lost, the catalogue preserved in the Potala calibrates the original influences shaping Tibet's own Buddhism and can be used to gauge the religion's spread within the country.

Tibet owes its literature to the all-pervasive practice of Buddhism. Learning and literacy were confined to the monastic orders and most monasteries encouraged the writing of biographies, drama, poetry, songs and ballads alongside learned words of canonical exegesis. Since Tibetan Buddhism sees the writing of a book as a religious act that can advance all those involved along the path to Nirvana, many books were commissioned or simply paid for by rich laymen concerned for their personal spiritual standing. The Potala's beautiful works represent a small part of the country's vast bibliographic inheritance.

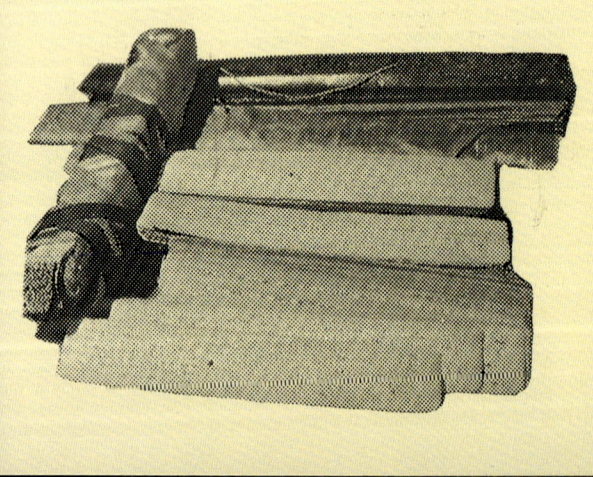

The Pattra Scriptures
The earliest Tibetan books were written on pattra palm leaves imported from India. These palm leaves are as fragile as papyrus or parchment and very few have survived the last millennium intact. Documents like those *right* provide the modern Tibetan scholar (*overleaf, top right*) with an invaluable source of information on the religious, cultural and socio-economic conditions of life in ancient days. Such pattra scriptures are reserved for serious scholastic study, but the occasional document is kept on show for its aesthetic beauty and historical value.

The Triptaka

The *Triptaka* is the name given to the vast canon of Tibetan Buddhist scriptures and their commentaries. The *Triptaka* is divided into two compendia, the *Kangyur* and the *Tangyur*, consisting of 208 and 224 volumes respectively, with a total of 4,569 works between them.

The *Kangyur* consists of the revealed wisdom of the Buddha Gautama and Sakyamuni's teachings. From the 18th century its 208 volumes were printed only in Nortang, Litang, Derge and Beijing. Volumes of the Beijing *Kangyur* were sometimes printed in gold (*left*) as a presentation edition for a Dalai, Panchen or other High Lama and frequently featured Sanskrit and Chinese texts in parallel to the Tibetan. Editions of the *Kangyur* from the Derge press may be distinguished by the red ink of their lettering.

The *Kangyur*'s language shows close affinities to the Sanskrit from which it was originally transcribed. This formality of language also distinguishes the *Tangyur*'s canonical volumes of exegesis and commentary. The *Tangyur* contains the works which have codified Tibetan art for the last six hundred years at least by setting forth strict guidelines as to the appearance and execution of any given theme or subject worthy of depiction. Other works contain information on arts and crafts, medicine and medical practice, history, astrology and theological dialectics. The works making up this cultural canon were first assembled in the 13th century and finally arranged in their definitive order in the middle of the 14th century by such monk-scholars as the famous Putston.

CHORTENS

The Red Palace was constructed as a mausoleum for the Great Fifth. Seven other Chorten Halls have been let into or added on to the original structure to provide resting places fit for the sacred remains of successive Dalai Lamas. Still preserved in their magnificent chortens or sarcophag are the remains of: Ngawang Lobzang Gyatso, the Grea Fifth; Keizang Gyatso, the 7th Dalai Lama; Jampe Gyatso, the 8th; Longto Gyatso, the 9th; Tshutrin Gyatso, the 10th; Khedon Gyatso, the 11th; Chinle Gyatso the 12th; and, lastly, Thutan Gyatso, Tibet's grea 13th Dalai Lama (Tsanyang Gyatso, the poetic 6th Dala Lama, was kidnapped from the Potala when Lhapsar Khan attacked Lhasa in 1705 and his murdered body was never recovered.)

All the Potala's chortens resemble one another in thei basic form which may be traced back to the stupas o ancient India. A massive rectangular base or plinth sup ports the spherical chamber with a latticed window let ting on to the salt-dried body preserved within (*overleaf left*). A large cone rises from this spherical middle and i itself capped by a bell engraved with images of the sun and the moon. This superstructure symbolizes the mos refined of the five elements, the ether of space; while the round middle symbolizes the element of air. The broac band at the base of the plinth represents the earth; and the element of water is signified in the plinth's broad middle bands, while the tiered sections rising up above this repre sent fire, and the last tier upon which the whole etherea structure rests represents the air.

Individual chortens vary greatly in both their size and in the magnificence of their ostentation. The very least o them is covered with gold and the most magnificent, the Great Fifth's, contains 110,000 ounces of gold. Each chor ten is lavishly decorated with pearls, jewels, precious and semi-precious stones most of which were contributed by the Tibetan people or sent as gifts from the courts o China, Nepal, Khotan, Bhutan, Sikkim and India.

Such munificence means that the Potala's chorten: represent a real vault of the wealth of the Tibetan Renais sance as well as a repository of its Lamaist culture. The foreign kings' gifts indicate the high international esteem in which Tibet's greatest religious leaders have always been held.

The 11th Dalai Lama's chorten (*opposite page*) displays the classical structure of all the Potala's chortens. Its surface is covered with beaten gold and inlaid with precious stones. The ethereal structure surrounding the Dalai Lama's body is especially lavish. The chorten's window diminishes the separation between the living and the dead, the worshipper and the object of his or her religious devotion. The detail *right* shows the window of the 13th Dalai Lama's chorten. Built in 1930 this chorten (*below*) is of solid silver coated with 18,800 ounces of gold, is richly studded with pearls, jade and jewellery, and rises through three storeys to 14 metres at its highest point.

Chorten Decorations
The Dalai Lamas' chortens are each decorated around the base with golden bas reliefs like the dragon (*right*). Many of the chortens are prettified with small precious ornaments like the *gawu* (*above*). The *gawu* is an amulet box which Tibetan women wore to ward off evil influences. It was not uncommon for women to donate such precious and powerful possessions to magnify the memory of a departed Dalai Lama.

Bas Relief
Dragons (*left*) and phoenixes (*below*) are the most common motifs decorating the Potala's eight chortens.

Three Dimensional Mandala
A mandala is normally a graphic, two dimensional symbol of the cosmos showing elaborate, symmetrical patterns placed on a square set within a circle bearing representations of Buddhist deities. Such mandalas are used as an aid to concentrate meditation. The mandala *above* was presented in homage to the 13th Dalai Lama's holy memory and is on display in his Chorten Hall. Its basic square and circular design is clear at a glance. Less obvious are the intricate designs and patterns set with no less than 200,000 pearls and coral pieces (*detail, opposite page*).

GOLDEN ROOFS

If Songtsan Gambo's Khritse Marpo is the Potala's original parent, then Princess Wen Cheng's Jokhang Temple must stand as its god-parent. The Potala's enchanting golden roofs owe more to the first Han influences in Tibetan Buddhism than they do to any drawings of Tibet's most ancient palaces. These roofs are a visual echo of the Jokhang's splendid pagoda which, until the Potala's roofing, was unique throughout Tibet.

The lovely gilded roofs rise from the Dalai Lamas' Chorten Halls below. Some few were constructed with gold generously granted for the purpose by the Qing emperors of the 18th century; all, however, owe more to the Han people than their gold. The craftsmanship of the Han artisans who helped build the Potala is nowhere more evident than in these roofs' upraised flying eaves with their projecting corners spouting fierce dragons and their sharp ridges sprouting lovely pagoda spires. The roofs' columns of gilded pillars embossed with Buddhist sutras and charms are as distinctively indigenous in origin as the bird deities holding down the many chains of tinkling prayer bells. Together with the roofs' gilt-rolled tiles and brass slates, these pillars, statues and charms glisten and glitter under the clear Lhasan sun and dazzle the eye.

Panorama
The magnificent roofing pavilion of the foregound belongs to the structure of the last Chorten Hall built on the 13th Dalai Lama's death in the Year of the Water Bird, 1933.

The Roofs at Sunset (*above*) are as lovely in their perfection now as they have ever been. At one time prayer flags would have flapped from the loops in the bells' clappers (*right*) and the bird deity would have stood firm above a forest of turning prayer wheels. Every toll of a bell, turn of a wheel or snap of a flag sent an inscribed prayer heavenwards.

The Gable End (*above*) is decorated with the *rtago-brgyad hum-gzugo*: this vase-shaped motif combines eight auspicious signs and is a common ornamentation of ritual objects or religious structures. The lotus at its base signifies religious purity; the two fish symbolize fidelity and the endless knot connecting the two motifs indicates eternity.

A Phoenix's Head (*detail right*) rises from the apex of a palace roof.

The Hectagonal Pavilion (*left*) is singular both for its unusual shape and for the flowerbuds which blossom from its corners. The dragon (*detail above*) is the decoration most commonly seen projecting from the Potala's topmost eaves.

At the Top: a woman and her child (*above*) delight in the panoramic view of Lhasa in its valley below (*right*).

Appendices

PLAN OF THE POTALA PALACE

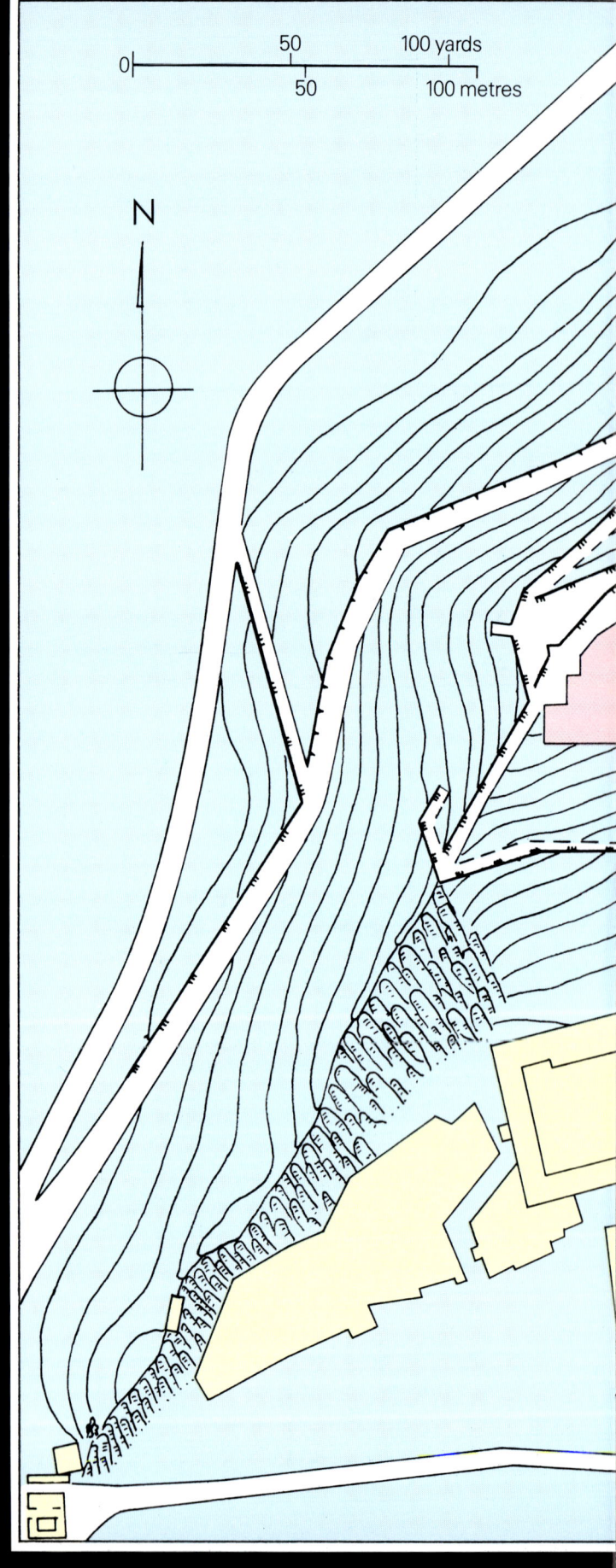

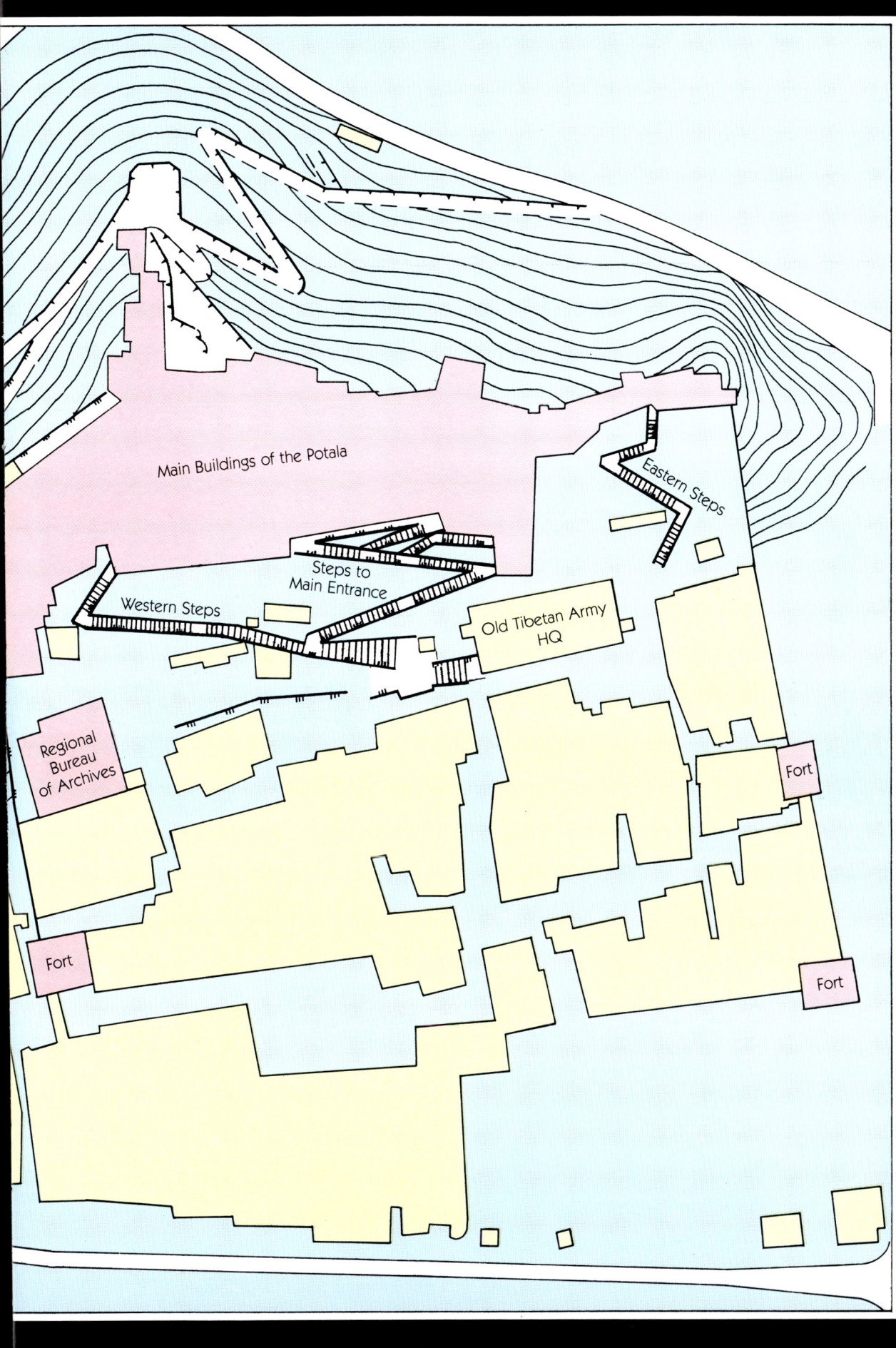

Main Buildings of the Potala

Eastern Steps

Steps to
Main Entrance

Western Steps

Old Tibetan Army
HQ

Regional
Bureau
of Archives

Fort

Fort

Fort

CHRONOLOGY OF THE POTALA

ANCIENT TIBET

634 A.D. – Year of the Horse, Tibetan Calendar
The Diplomatic Mission sent by King Songtsan Gambo of Tibet arrives in Chang'an and requests the hand of a Tang Princess in marriage to the Tibetan *tsanpo* (King). The Tang Emperor sends a reciprocal Diplomatic Mission to Lhasa, the city where earlier in the century Songtsan Gambo had established the seat of his government. Recognition of the Tubo dynasty's rule over Tibet.

641, Year of the Ox
The Tang Princess Wen Cheng arrives in Lhasa to be married to the Tibetan King. She is installed in the Khritse Marpo (Palace of the Red Canopied Throne) that Songtsan Gambo constructed for her on the Marpo Ri (Red Hill) outside Lhasa.

710, Year of the Dog
The Tang Princess Jin Cheng arrives in Lhasa to be married to King Khride Tsutsan.

755, Year of the Sheep
The accession of Khride Tsutsan's and Jin Cheng's son, Khrisong Detsan, as King of Tibet. Sometime during his reign the Khritse Marpo is badly damaged by lightning.

842, Year of the Male Water Dog
The assassination of Tsanpo Lang Darma occurs during the general uprising which destroys the Khritse Marpo and ends the Tubo dynasty's rule of the country.

RENAISSANCE TIBET

1645, Year of the Female Woodcock
The 5th Dalai Lama, Ngawang Lobzang Gyatso, begins to build the Potala's White Palace on the Marpo Ri.

1653, Year of the Female Water Snake
The 5th Dalai Lama visits the Qing Emperor in Beijing. Emperor Shun Zhi confers on Ngawang Lobzang Gyatso the title: 'The Great Benevolent Self-Existent Buddha of Western Paradise, Overseer of the Buddhist Faith under Heaven, the All-Knowing Vadjradhara Dalai Lama'. The Dalai Lama moves from his Gandan Phodrang Palace in the Drepung Monastery to the Zimchung Nyierh (the Sunlight Halls) in the Potala's White Palace.

1690, Year of the Male Iron Horse
The Depa (Dalai Lama's Regent) Sanggye Gyatso begins work on the Potala's Red Palace. This building is designed as a mausoleum to the 5th Dalai Lama who actually died some eight to eleven years before. The Red Palace is completed three years later.

1697, Year of the Female Fire Ox
The installation of Tsanyang Gyatso (1683-1706) as Tibet's 6th Dalai Lama.

1706, Year of the Male Fire Dog
The leader of the Qosot Mongols, Lhazang Khan, kills Sanggye Gyatso and abducts the 6th Dalai Lama who dies in mysterious circumstances. Yeshi Gyatso (the false 7th) is placed on the Lion Throne and promoted as Tibet's Dalai Lama. This leads to great unrest and in 1709 the Qing Emperor, Kang Xi, sends a ministerial official from Beijing to try and resolve the situation. Little is accomplished and the situation worsens. In 1717 the Jungar Mongols invade Tibet, capture Lhasa and kill Lhazang Khan. In the following year Kang Xi sends an army to oust the Mongols and by 1719-20 Tibet is freed from their presence and order is restored.

1720, Year of the Male Iron Mouse
The installation of Keizang Gyatso (1708-1757) as Tibet's true 7th Dalai Lama. Two Ambans are established in Lhasa.

1762, Year of the Male Water Horse
An Amban presides at the installation of Jampei Gyatso (1758-1804) as Tibet's 8th Dalai Lama.

1808, Year of the Male Earth Dragon
An Amban presides at the installation of Longto Gyatso (1805-1815) as Tibet's 9th Dalai Lama.

1822, Year of the Male Earth Horse
An Amban presides at the installation of Tshutrim Gyatso (1816-1837) as Tibet's 10th Dalai Lama.

1842, Year of the Male Earth Tiger
An Amban presides at the installation of Khedon Gyatso (1838-1855) as Tibet's 11th Dalai Lama.

1858, Year of the Male Earth Horse
An Amban presides at the installation of Chinlei Gyatso (1856-1875) as Tibet's 12th Dalai Lama.

1878, Year of the Male Earth Tiger
Installation of Thutan Gyatso (1876-1933) as Tibet's 13th Dalai Lama.

1904, Year of the Male Wood Dragon
The British invading force commanded by Colonel Younghusband fights off Tibetan resistance to its advance on Lhasa and holds the city until the 'Lhasa Convention' is finally signed.

SELECTED BIBLIOGRAPHY

MODERN TIBET

1934, Year of the Male Wood Dog
The Chief Commissioner of the Commission on Mongolian and Tibetan Affairs conveys condolences on the 13th Dalai Lama's death and awards him posthumous honours. The 13th Dalai Lama's chorten is begun at the Potala and is eventually completed two years later.

1940, Year of the Male Iron Dragon
The Chief Commissioner of the Commission on Mongolian and Tibetan Affairs supervises the installation of Tandzin Gyatso (1935-present) as Tibet's 14th Dalai Lama.

1951, Year of the Female Iron Hare
Representatives of the Central People's Government and Tibetan officials conclude the agreement confirming Tibet as an Autonomous Region within the People's Republic of China. In 1961 the Central Government declares the Potala a state historical monument enjoying national protection.

Compiled by Chang Fengxuan

Born in Yuci, Shanxi in 1927, Chang Fengxuan is of the Han nationality.

He studied at China University and at Peking University and graduated from the National Minority Languages Department of the Central Nationalities College.

He is now an assistant research fellow of the National Research Institute of the Chinese Academy of Social Science.

Bell, Sir Charles. *Tibet Past and Present*, Oxford University Press, 1924

Chapman, F. Spencer. *Lhasa: The Holy City*, London, 1938

Combe, G.A. *A Tibetan on Tibet*, London, 1926

Eberhard, W. *Kultur und Siedlung der Randvolker Chinas*, Leiden, 1942

Gordon, A.K. *The Iconography of Tibetan Lamaism,* 2nd edn., Rutland (Vermont) and Tokyo, 1959

Harrer, Heinrich. *Seven Years in Tibet*, London, 1953

Hopkirk, Peter. *Trespassers on the Roof of the World: The Race for Lhasa*, London, 1982

Kling, Kevin. *Tibet*, London, 1985

Macdonald, D. *The Land of the Lama*, London, 1929

Monod-Bruhl, O. *Peintures tibetaines*, Paris, 1954

Richardson, Hugh E. *Tibet and its History,* 2nd edn., Boulder, Colorado and London, 1984

Rowell, Galen. *Mountains of the Middle Kingdom: Exploring the High Peaks of China and Tibet*, London, 1985

Shen, T.L. and Liu, S.C. *Tibet and the Tibetans*, Stanford, 1953

Stein, R.A. *La Civilisation tibetaine*, Paris, 1962

Suyin, Han. *The Open City: A Journey to Lhasa*, London, 1977

Tafel, Dr. Albert. *Meine Tibetreise, Eine Studienfahrt durch das nordwestliche China und durch die innere Mongolei in des ostliche Tibet, Bande 1 und 11*, Stuttgart, Berlin, Leipzig, 1914

Tandzin Gyatso, His Holiness the Dalai Lama. *My Land and My People*, London, 1962

Younghusband, Francis. *India and Tibet*, London, 1910

Zahiruddin, Ahmad. *Sino-Tibetan Relations in the Seventeenth Century*, Rome, 1970

THE POTALA DESCRIBED ~1

by Deng Ruiling

THE POTALA PALACE, situated on the Red Hill in the north-west of the Municipality of Lhasa, People's Republic of China, is the largest and the best preserved monument of ancient Tibetan architecture extant today. Covering the whole face of the hill from its foot at more than 3,600 metres above sea level, the main portion of the building rises in thirteen storeys to more than 110 metres in height, and the whole edifice measures well over 360 metres in width. Built entirely of wood and stone, this immense towering structure comprises a maze of rooms and compartments heaped up in seeming irregularity and intricate workmanship. Crowned with glistening golden roofs and soaring eaves, it is surrounded by steep walls overhanging flights of stone steps winding to the gates. When viewed from a distance, the whole complex presents an impressive picture of harmony, grandeur and magnificence beyond description. Truly it is a masterpiece of Tibetan architectural beauty and an embodiment of the creative genius of the Tibetan working people.

The Potala Palace was built in the middle of the 17th century by order of a great personage in Tibetan history, the 5th Dalai Lama, Ngawang Lobzang Gyatso. According to records, construction work began in the Year of the Wood Cock of the 11th Rabjune (a Rabjune is a sixty-year cycle in the Tibetan calendar), i.e., 1645 A.D. This was the fourth year after the 5th Dalai Lama, as the head of the Gelukpa sect and with the military aid of the Qosot Mongols from Qinghai, had vanquished his rival and supporter of the Karmapa sect, the Tsangpa Khan of Tsang. It took fully three years to complete the part of the building known as the White Palace to which he removed from the Drepung Monastery. Ever since, the White Palace has become the official residence of all his successors.

Potala, a phonetic translation of the Sanskrit *Potalaka*, is the name of a hill on the southern coast of ancient India. Monk Xuan Zhuang of the Tang dynasty more accurately transcribed it in his *Records on the West Regions of the Tang Dynasty (Datang xiyu ji)*, in which he gave not only an account of its topographical features but also the myth that the Boddhisattva Avalokitesvara used to make it a place of his sojourn. And as the abode of the said Boddhisattva, the name in translation was further contracted to *Po Tuo*. According to the Tibetan historical work *A Happy Feast of Sages (Mkhas ba'i dga' stor)*, it was King Songtsan Gambo who first built a fort-palace on the Red Hill. As Tibetan Buddhists traditionally regarded him as the incarnation of Boddhisattva Avalokitesvara, the hill came to be known as 'Potala'. And according to *The Precious Tree of Perfect Bliss (Dpag bsam ljon bZang)* by Sumpa Khanpo, the fort-palace was once destroyed by thunder in the time of King Khrisong Detsan. Hence, the present palace was rebuilt on the ruins of the old site of the 7th century.

Now in choosing a site of such historical background for reconstruction the 5th Dalai Lama proved himself a man of subtle political acumen. Since there had been in Tibet the old tradition about Songtsan Gambo being the incarnation of the Boddhisattva, he was thus emulating the historical significance of the famous king. And by restoring the palace at Potala, the alleged abode of the Boddhisattva, he was comparing his own efforts in subduing the remnant Karmapa sect and in unifying U, Tsang and Ngari with the illustrious deeds of the founder of the Tubo dynasty by the implication that they were actually 'the two merged in one.' Thus the palace was destined to be not only a hermit-age for retirement and meditation of the head of a religious sect but also a centre for the feudal government of Tibet during the last three hundred years or more.

The Red Palace which forms the central portion of the whole structure was mainly built between 1690 and 1693 under Depa Sanggye Gyatso. It was built in the memory of the 5th Dalai Lama after his decease. And here is ensconced the huge chorten wherein his remains were preserved.

The construction of the whole palace lasting over several decades may be said to have been completed in the main by the end of the 17th century. It was estimated that seven thousand artisans took part in the building of the Red Palace alone, while those employed in hewing timbers and stones from the forest and quarry were to be counted in tens of thousands. This gives a sufficient idea of the magnitude of corvée labour and material resource used to be exacted from the people by the 5th Dalai Lama and Sanggye Gyatso, backed as they were by both the central authority of the Qing dynasty and the military prowess of the Qosot Mongols. It also indicates, nonetheless, a thriving social economy under stable political unity which made it possible for the people to supply the necessary manpower and resource over such a long period.

At that time there were also monk artisans of Han nationality who came from inland to join in the planning and construction. So while the basic structure of the palace is a combination of a residence and a fort, which accords with the Tibetan tradition, it has also assimilated many decorative features, including the elaborate beams and rafters, corbel brackets, gold roofings, painted ceilings, etc., characteristic of Han architecture.

In the numerous corridors and porticos, mural paintings done by the famous Tibetan artists vividly portray scenes of the toiling mass while construction was in progress, leaving us a most valuable and authentic record of the history of the palace.

In 1661 A.D., when the 5th Dalai Lama was just at the zenith of his power, the Jesuit Father Grueber and his companion travelled from Beijing to Lhasa via Qinghai. As the Potala then consisted of only the White Palace, he left behind a sketch of it as he saw it, perhaps the first sketch ever made. Fifty-five years later, another Jesuit missionary named Desideri arrived at Lhasa, and he noticed that the palace comprised both the White Palace and the Red Palace. This was what he wrote: 'Now this palace occupies the whole top of the rock of Potala, but in the old days it was smaller, as shown by the drawing made by the Rev. Albert D'Orville and Rev. Johan Grueber of our society . . .'

In the time of the Emperor Kang Xi, many Han artisans participated in the construction of the palace and many imperial envoys must have left their footprints on the stone steps leading to the White Palace. But it was in 1720 that a military officer named Li Fengcai in the expedition force to expel the Jungar Mongols from Lhasa explicitly mentioned Potala as the name of the place where the Living Buddha was enthroned, with a description of its fearful images of worship and its treasures overflowing with wealth. A contemporary civil officer, Jiao Yingqi, after a short stay of eight days in Lhasa also remarked in his journals about the Dalai Lama's magnificent palace with words like "Hundreds of towering buildings, many storeys high, with beautiful adornments in shining gold that defy description", though he did not mention its name.

Since the time of Sanggye Gyatso, the palace had been extended by successive generations of Dalai Lamas especially in the 18th century. And since it was the residence of Dalai Lamas and the administrative centre of the Tibet Region, important religious ceremonies and festivals took place here every year. All important political functions were also held here such as the formal instalation of each young Dalai Lama when the Resident Amban of the Qing court presided over the ceremony in the East Hall to inaugurate the Dalai into office. Imperial edicts, royal letters of appointment, gold diplomas and gold seals issued by the Central Government to the high clerical and lay officials together with religious utensils and plaques bearing the Emperor's handwriting were preserved here, as was also the memorial tablet dedicated to the Emperor in the four languages of Han, Tibetan, Manchurian and Mongolian. All these bear testimony to the authority vested in the Tibetan leadership headed by the Dalai Lama and ratified by the Central Government as to their being legitimate rulers of Tibet.

In the White Palace, the Dalai Lama and his clerical attendants lived, prayed and supervised the daily administration, while the main part of the Red Palace is reserved, among a number of prayer halls, for the eight chortens covered with shining gold, pearls and gems in which the embalmed bodies of the deceased Dalai Lamas were preserved.

Potala is also a veritable museum of the arts, the best talents of Tibet being represented here in sculpture, painting, printing, calligraphy and other fine arts and crafts. Especially valuable are the mural paintings in the numerous corridors and porticos. There are paintings on religious subjects as well as scenes from the daily life of the Tibetan people. Fine pictures about the story of the Princesses Wen Cheng and Jin Cheng of the Tang dynasty are to be seen in the corridors and the East Audience Hall of the White Palace, demonstrating the genuine affection of the Tibetan people for the two princesses who devoted themselves to promoting cultural exchange and harmonious relation between the Han and Tibetan nationalities. In the West Audience Hall are paintings depicting the audience granted by the Qing Emperor Shun Zhi to the 5th Dalai Lama at Beijing and that of Emperor Guang Xu and Empress Dowager Ci Xi to the 13th Dalai Lama, indicating the Dalai Lamas' subordination to the Emperors.

Towards the end of the 19th century, the Potala like many other places of historical importance in China experienced defilement by imperialism. In the year 1904, it was in the main hall of the Potala Palace that, under the threat of British military power, Tibetan officials were forced to sign the 'Lhasa Convention'.

This imposing structure on the Red Hill had stood as a historical witness to the many political vicissitudes which Tibet had gone through in the past till the day of democratic reform. Now, cleansed of all stains of its former humiliation, tyranny and iniquity, it is restored to the people.

Since liberation, the State Council of the People's Republic of China has given the greatest attention to this world-renowned old Tibetan architecture and allocated special funds every year for its repair and maintenance. In 1961, Potala was officially declared one of the old historical sites under state protection. It is now a unique historical museum and is drawing an ever increasing number of visitors, both native and foreign, to come each year.

Reprinted at the request of the People's Art Publishing House, Shanghai.

Deng Ruiling, of the Manchu nationality, was born in Beijing in 1925.
He graduated from the History Dept. and later from the Research Institute of Peking University.
He is now an assistant research fellow of the Nationality Research Institute of the Chinese Academy of Social Sciences. His present position is Deputy Director of the Research Centre of the Institute.

THE POTALA DESCRIBED~2

by Dongar Lobzand Chinlei
Translated from Tibetan by Trashi Wangdu & Chang Fengxuan

THE POTALA PALACE is the creation of the industrious and ingenious Tibetan working people who successfully employed their remarkable cultural and artistic heritage. It embodies in itself the technical and artistic accomplishments of civil engineering, palatial layout, sculpture, casting, mural painting and interior decoration of Tibetan culture and is one of the wonders among the world's buildings.

The palace is a gigantic architectural structure built in the traditional Tibetan style, with a history of over 1,000 years. In the early 7th century, the wise *tsanpo* (king) Songstan Gambo (617-650, unifier and first king of unified Tibet) came of age and took the reigns of government. He built a house on the Marpo Ri (Red Hill) shaped like a sleeping elephant. This was later to become the Chogye Drupha (Meditation Palace for the Religious Lords), situated at the northern part of the hill. Songstan Gambo took to wife a Nepalese and a Han princess. When Princess Wen Cheng from the Tang Court was on her way to Tibet, he built another palace on the Marpo Ri, and named it the Khritse Marpo (Palace of the Red-Canopied Throne), or the Potala (Abode of Avalokitesvara). This is how the Potala came into being according to historical records. The Red Palace, as it was later called, was damaged during the reign of Mangsong Mangtsan, and later was destroyed by lightning fire during the reign of Khrisong Detsan in the 8th century. But a picture of the Red Palace is preserved intact in a fresco inside the main entrance of the Jokhang Temple in Lhasa.

After this, Tibet experienced a long period of turmoil and war, and the palaces became run-down and dilapidated. During the 12th century, Kardampa Geshay preached Buddhist scriptures on the Potala Hill, and afterwards, Master Tsong Khapa, the founder of the Karmapa and Gelukpa of Tshurphu, also gave sermons on Buddhist sutras there. Obviously, the buildings on top of the hill were no longer palaces at the time, but houses for preaching Buddhism. During the consecutive rules of Phamo Drupa and Karmapa of the Kargyupa sect over U (Anterior Tibet), temporary imperial palaces were set up in Lhasa. Ngawang Trashi Drapa, the 11th king of the Phadru Dynasty, built a temporary imperial residence the Gangri Karpo (Palace of the Snow-Capped Mountain) in Qüsü, thus guarding the strategic point overlooking the regions of U, Tsang and Lhoka. He gave his former residence, Dokhang Ngenmo (Green Rock Palace) in the Drepung Monastery, to the 2nd Dalai Lama. Later, the Dalai Lama changed the name of the Dokhang Ngenmo into the Gandan Phodrang, which became the holy residence of the 2nd, 3rd, 4th and 5th Dalai Lamas.

In early 17th century, the Qosot tribe of the Oelot Mongols invaded Tibet. They overthrew Karma Tanhwei Wangpu and helped the 5th Dalai Lama to the throne. The 5th Dalai Lama found that living in the Gandan Phodrang Palace within the Drepung Monastery was an infringement of the regulations of the monastery. But he also considered the Gangri Karpo Palace in Qüsü too far away from the three great monasteries in Lhasa. Therefore he built, in 1645-1648, a new palace on the eastern side of the Potala Hill according to the design of the Red Palace of Songstan Gambo as preserved in the fresco in the Jokhang temple. He named the new palace the White Palace. The reason for choosing the Potala Hill as the site for his new palace was that it was the place where Songstan Gambo set up his first government after unifying Tibet, and it was there that Songstan Gambo married the Nepalese

princess and Princess Wen Cheng from the Tang Court. Furthermore, it was situated at the place which for centuries had been the centre of friendly exchange in political, economic and cultural fields among various nationalities. The Potala was within easy reach of the three great monasteries of Lhasa, and, therefore, convenient for keeping a tight hold on the state and the church. So, after the completion of the White Palace, the 5th Dalai Lama moved his residence from the Gandan Phodrang Palace in the Drepung Monastery to the Zimchung Nyierh Palace (Sunlight Palace) on top of the Potala Hill. From then on, this palace has been the living quarters of successive Dalai Lamas. The Audience Hall on the ground floor of the White Palace was the place where various Dalai Lamas attended to state and church affairs. The frescoes in this hall, which still retain their bright colours, were painted by Choying Gyatso, a famous painter sent by the 4th Panchen Lama from the Trashi Lhumpo Monastery. The palace also housed the Kashag (the Council of Ministers) and the Yitsang (the Secretariat) set up during the early years of the Qing Dynasty. The White Palace was kept in good repair and underwent several renovations during the reigns of the 8th, 9th, 12th and 13th Dalai Lamas.

The central part of the Potala Palace is the Red Palace. It was built under the general supervision of Depa (Chief Administrator) Sanggye Gyatso. Construction work began in 1690, the Year of the Iron Horse in the Tibetan calendar, eight years after the death of the 5th Dalai Lama. It took four years to complete the work. The builders tore down half of the western part of the original White Palace and extended the former Red Palace on its eastern, southern and western sides. Conforming to the Tibetan tradition, the palace has thirteen storeys and bears the features of both palaces and temples in its outward appearance; while the interior was built strictly according to the design of Tantric cosmography.

The top floor of the Red Palace, decorated in conformity with the design of the orthodox Gelukpa sect, was the living quarters of the Dalai Lama. The floor below includes the Hall of the Medicine King, the Lama Hall, the Hall of the God of the Hans, the Hall of the Bronze Buddha of Khotan, etc. Further below are the Prayer Hall and four other great halls at its four sides. The walls of the Prayer Hall are decorated with frescoes depicting the life story of the 5th Dalai Lama. On the walls of the corridor outside the Prayer Hall are frescoes presenting the life of Depa Sanggye Gyatso. Frescoes are also found in other halls telling the life stories of Masters Atisha and Dromtonpa, teacher and disciple, of the Gelukpa sect. These frescoes were painted by Tandzin Norbu and other Tibetan master painters of the time. Apart from the eight chortens containing salt-dried and embalmed remains of eight Dalai Lamas, there are preserved in the palace 246 scrolls of paintings in gold, 65 colour scrolls depicting the life story of the 5th Dalai Lama, 46 privately handed-down scrolls, 615 Buddhist sutras in gold characters, the *Kangyur* and the *Tangyur*, also gold-charactered, and other valuable books on medicine, calendar and history as well as biographies and anthologies.

In building the Red Palace craftsmen of many trades were employed; among them are painters, engravers, founders, mosaicists, goldsmiths, coppersmiths, ironsmiths, spinners, tanners, greasers, mortar mixers and stonemasons. The authorities also enlisted corvée labourers from serfs of the households of seven high-ranking officials, thirteen aristocratic households and monastic plantations. Craftsmen of Han, Mongolian and Nepalese nationalities were invited to participate in this grandiose project. According to historical records, a total of 6,743 Tibetan, Han, Mongolian and Nepalese craftsmen worked jointly in building this magnificent and awe-inspiring palace in traditional Tibetan architectural style.

The layout of the palace was done with superb skill that puts nature to shame. It is a building complex in which the White and Red Palaces are ingeniously grouped together. After nearly three hundred years, the palace is still in good condition, magnificent and splendid as ever. Obviously, without a period of political solidarity and stability and a fairly developed economy, it would be impossible to launch such a giant undertaking. After the peaceful liberation of the Tibetan Region, the people's government listed the Potala Palace among the first class of cultural relics to be put under state protection. Large funds are allocated every year by the state for the repair and renovation of the Potala.

The Potala Palace is admired by people of all nationalities in China. It is the fruit of the collective intelligence of many brilliant statesmen, clever craftsmen and industrious working people of different historical periods. It is the pride of the Chinese nation.

Reprinted at the request of the People's Art Publishing House, Shanghai.

Dongar Lobzand Chinlei, born in Milin County of the Tibetan Autonomous Region in 1927, is of the Tibetan nationality. He is the living Buddha of the Dongar Monastery in Gongbu Region of Tibet. He once studied in Sela Monastery of Lhasa and was awarded the title of dge-bshes *(equivalent to a doctoral degree in Buddhism) after passing the final examination and meanwhile was awarded the degrees of* Lha-rim-pa *and* Sngags-rim-pa *of the Tri-monasteries.*

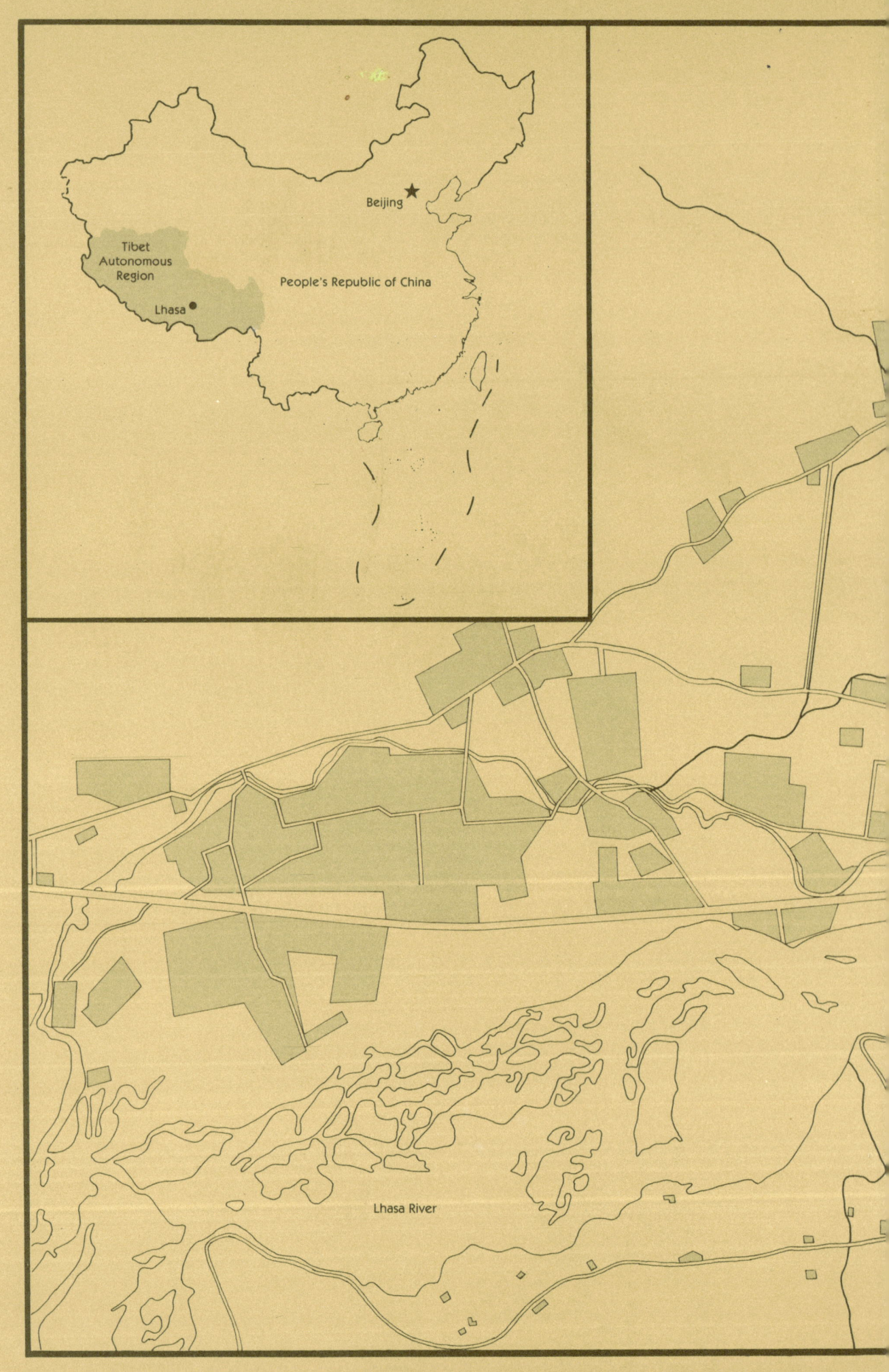

Tibet
Autonomous
Region

Lhasa

People's Republic of China

Beijing

Lhasa River